MW01257412

Bet On Yourself

Bet On Yourself

INSIDE THE MIND OF THE
ULTIMATE UNDERDOG

Antoine Bethea
with *Terez Paylor*

AB41 PUBLISHING LLC

For information about special discounts for bulk purchases or to book an event, please visit our website at www.antoinebethea.com.

Book Cover Design by Cat Peoples
Book Cover Photography by Clifton Prescod

Library of Congress Cataloging-In-Publication Data has been applied for.

ISBN 978-0-9980448-0-4
ISBN 978-0-9980448-2-8 (eBook)
ISBN 978-0-9980448-1-1 (Hardcover)

Printed in the United States of America

lu·mi·nar·y
*a person who inspires or influences others, especially one prominent
in a particular sphere*

*This book is dedicated to all of my underdogs fighting to prove
themselves every day*

Lineup

Foreword

ANTOINE BETHEA IS ONE OF the great success stories in NFL history.

I first saw him playing three-deep single safety at Howard University, which is not a traditional, big-time football power. I took the tape to Tony Dungy and said, "I think this young man can play cornerback for us, but you're the expert, please take a look." Tony did and said, "He can play for us. Let's get him. We'll start him at safety where he will be comfortable and after a break-in period, we will move him to corner where he will flourish."

We never said a word to anyone else about Antoine prior to the draft. Our luck held and we got him in the sixth round. He came to mini-camp with the veterans as an unknown fourth stringer. In the first practice—interception! In the second practice—interception! Prior to the third practice, Antoine was moved to second string and Peyton Manning said, "Who is the kid making all those plays?" In the third practice against the number one offense—interception! After Antoine's third pick, Coach Dungy came up to me and said, "I think we'll leave him at safety." So we did, and he has been there for thirteen outstanding seasons with the Colts, 49ers and Cardinals.

Why? How? Very simple. There have been few players who have ever prepared twelve months a year mentally, physically, and emotionally with the dedication evidenced by Antoine. He became a starter during his rookie mini-camp but continues, to this day, to prepare as though he is still a rookie striving to make the team. All that hard work and dedication has led Antoine to be the epitome of Coach Dungy's phrase "Quiet Strength!" Antoine Bethea is a "Pro's Pro," someone revered by his teammates, respected by opponents, and beloved by coaches, GMs, and owners. He speaks at length publicly for the first time in this book, and when you read this story and meet him through these pages, I know you will appreciate this sentiment I have often stated: "What a lucky day for the Colts and me personally when Antoine became one of us." It was a joy to be his teammate and friend, and an honor to commend this book to you.

— Bill Polian

Prologue

"The Super Bowl champs are in the building!"

I'll never forget the chills that reverberated through my body when the D.J. shouted that on the morning of February 5, 2006, and I'll certainly never forget the way all eyes in the dark nightclub seemed to shift toward me and my teammates at that very moment.

It was about 2 a.m. or so, and we were definitely living the good life, just dancing, drinking, and laughing at a nightclub in Miami. Just hours earlier, we had beaten the Chicago Bears 29-17 in Super Bowl XLI to ascend to the top of the professional football world. The euphoria was all over our faces.

Some guys chose to celebrate this monumental achievement in a little quieter fashion; at dinner with their families, for instance. But I was 22 years young and ready to party, so I joined about 30 to 40 teammates at the club to celebrate a victory that was sweeter than I ever could have imagined.

Between the champagne and the confidence that comes with knowing you just outlasted 31 other teams to win football's ultimate prize, we were the life of the party. It was crazy that night; beautiful women were everywhere, congratulating us at every turn. Between the laughter and the fellowship, we all basically kept looking at each other like, wow, so this is what it feels like to be a Super Bowl champion!

It was the kind of scene that, to be honest, would make anyone wonder just how in the hell they got there. I always saw myself as an underdog, and I know for a fact I wasn't the only one who saw me that way. Only five years earlier, there was no way that anyone—*anyone*—would have thought that Antoine Bethea, a no-star high school senior from Newport News, Va., who basically had to walk-on at Division 1-AA Howard University, would be a Super Bowl champion, let alone a rookie starter the entire season.

But I wasn't really thinking about the "hows" and the "whys" then. I was conscious that this moment was special, but I didn't dwell on the journey, if that makes any sense. In that moment, all I knew was that the drinks were flowing, the people were friendly, and by God, we were going to celebrate this achievement until the sun came up. This was my reward for making it against all odds, and there was no way in hell I was letting this night end before it had to.

The funny thing about winning the Super Bowl as a longshot is, after the initial high of winning it all—which lasts several months, if you're celebrating it properly—as long as you're a professional football player, you never stop chasing that feeling again. You begin to wonder, slowly but surely, how you did it. Then the euphoria of it all wears off little by little, day by day, until the next season rolls around and all of a sudden, you're sweating your ass off during a May practice, wondering where the hell time went, while a coach barks orders at you.

Interestingly enough, I began to find that other people loved to ask me how I did it, too. That continued to happen to me even four months after we won it all, like the night we received our championship rings during a private team ceremony in June, for instance.

I remember sitting at a table in the ballroom of a theater in downtown Indianapolis, taking it all in as the highlights of our Super Bowl season ran on a giant screen. There was a square dance floor in the middle of the ballroom, which was lit with blue and white lights to match our team colors. There was even a massive ice sculpture with the Colts horseshoe in the corner.

This setup is really nice—a fitting setting for a coronation, I thought to myself.

Sinbad, the comedian, was emceeing, and after he cracked a few jokes, our head coach, Tony Dungy, spoke, and so did our team owner, Mr. Jim Irsay, and our general manager, Bill Polian. Our star quarterback, Peyton Manning, spoke, too. It was around this time that my big brother, Alexon—who I invited as my plus-one—summed up my journey to that point pretty succinctly.

"Yo, you're really about to get a Super Bowl ring," he turned and said to me with no shortage of wonder. "From Denbigh High School to Howard University to Super Bowl champion your rookie year …. this is crazy. Did you ever think this would happen?"

I remember looking at him—a bit tipsy from the celebratory spirits, I admit—and smiling.

"Naw man," I said, shaking my head. "I don't think anybody did."

I was still a young man at the time, and I'm not gonna lie, I was too busy enjoying my come-up to fully ponder on a question like that. Hell, I still had a whole career to play, and anyway, I was more concerned about the party that loomed later on that night at Club Six in Indianapolis, and how much fun that was going to be.

But eventually, when we received our championship rings, the weight of the achievement really started to hit me. I closely studied the ring, which featured white diamonds surrounding a Colts logo filled with blue sapphires. My name, Bethea, was on one side, along with the Colts horseshoe. On the other side, you had the score of the win over the Bears (29-17) above the word "Faith," a nod to the faith our team had in one another and how some coaches and players had faith dealing with personal situations off the field.

There was also a ruby in the ring, one that signified the blood, sweat, and tears we all put in to make that dream a reality. And as I slipped it on for the first time that night, it really began to hit me how far I'd come.

In the years that followed, as I grew older and became one of the old heads in the locker room, I began to reflect on my journey more and more, especially when I tried to counsel young players just entering the league. What did I do that worked? What did I do that didn't work? I liked the thought of being a positive locker room presence, a guy who paid it forward, just like all the vets on the Colts had once done with me.

My thoughts on this journey only became clearer as I spoke to college and high school students and their parents. It seemed like the more I shared pieces of my experience, the more their curiosity grew about my story.

So now, here I am, doing just that. I hope it inspires you, because I don't think I'm different by any means. After 13 years in the NFL, I realize I'm just an ordinary guy who had the good fortune (in retrospect) to go through a multitude of events that taught me some important lessons that helped me stare down the trials and tribulations life threw at me as I got older.

And believe me, when it comes to tough times, I've been through a few. When I was a child, I was deeply impacted by three of my loved ones' showdowns with death, not all of which ended positively. When I was a high school senior, my dream of using college to earn a full ride and get out of Newport News looked hopeless when, as a 5-foot-11, 170-pound linebacker, not a single Division 1 or Division 2 school offered me a scholarship before graduation.

Then, when I somehow managed to turn myself into an NFL Draft prospect anyway, I again had my dream of making the NFL repeatedly tested during a drama-filled process that included a draft-day surprise and one particularly miserable pre-draft experience with an NFL scout that had me questioning if I was in over my head.

And finally, when I made it to the NFL in spite of all that and still hit it big—starting for a Super Bowl champion as a rookie—I'd soon find out that was just the start of a never-ending string of tests that taught me the importance of surrounding myself with good people, never losing my edge and always standing for what I believed in, all in the name of keeping everything I'd earned to that point.

Looking back, I realize that everything I've gone through in my life has required me to either learn a vital lesson or institute one I'd already learned in the past just to get through it, and it is my desire to share those lessons with you, in hopes that you—no matter your age, race, gender, or profession—can take something from my experiences and perhaps use them in your own life to accomplish your goals. Life is often unfair, and being an adult is hard; the way I see it, we're all underdogs in this world.

But the good news is, if Antoine Bethea, a 5-foot-nothing high school linebacker can somehow go on to play 13 years in the NFL as a safety and make three Pro Bowls, then trust me, you can make your dreams come true, too, whatever they are, as long as you quiet the noise of naysayers, rid yourself of fear, doubt, and frustration and—of course—decide to bet on yourself.

Tomorrow isn't Promised

As I GLANCED DOWN AT my shoes while walking through the doors of the Naval Medical Center, my eight-year old self was nervous and uneasy, completely unsure of what to expect.

My mother, Verina Bethea, was in the recovery unit—that much I knew. And my father, Larry—a strong, silent type who was perhaps wary of telling me too much at the time—said little as we walked down the corridor with my 16-year-old brother, Alexon, to my mother's room.

I took deep breaths as we drew near, anxious to see my mom. But nothing could have prepared me for what awaited on the other side of that door, a sight that nearly made my heart fall out of my chest.

My mother's head was wrapped with white bandages, and her face was badly swollen. Her forehead and cheeks were a reddish purple, protruding enough to make her eyes look like marbles. To be honest, she looked like she had been beaten pretty badly. I hardly recognized her.

Within seconds, I felt a mixture of confusion and fear rise from the pit of my stomach to my eye ducts, and soon, the tears started pouring out in a way both my eight-year-old self—and even my mother—were completely unaccustomed to.

"Baby, I'm okay," she told me, softly. "I'm gonna be alright."

But she sure didn't look that way, and I sure as hell didn't feel that way. As the doctor watched the concern grow stronger over my face, he politely interjected.

"Maybe you want to take him outside the room right now, let him settle down," he said.

Prior to that day—which was the first of three incidents that would set me toward the path of comprehending my first rule to overcoming the odds—I'd say I lived a pretty standard life, one with little drama.

My mom and dad were high school sweethearts. They grew up in Lake View, South Carolina, where they attended the local black elementary school because of segregation. Then they went to the all-black high school, Columbus, which ended up merging with the white high school to create Lake View High School while they were students there.

To give you an idea of how charismatic my pops was, he was the senior class president, despite the fact the school had just been integrated. He was an athlete, at 5 feet 11 and a rock-solid 200-plus pounds, and a star football and basketball player. My mom was a majorette, and they started dating their senior year in high school.

My dad went on to attend the University of South Carolina for a short time. In 1976, my brother Alexon was born, and my mom and dad got married November 5, 1977. This is when my dad had to make a decision and ended up joining the military. I was born eight years later, 1984, in Savannah, Georgia, where my dad was stationed at the time, but my earliest memories as a kid were in Mannheim, Germany, where he was later stationed.

That's when I remember my parents really starting to drill home the importance of discipline. There was no talking back to either of them, and if my mom asked you something, you didn't say "yeah" or "no." You said "Yes ma'am, no ma'am." I still do that to this day when addressing authority figures, even though I'm well into my 30s and you don't hear people saying that as much these days. People definitely look at you a little different when you say that as a 34-year-old man, but that's just how I was raised.

We eventually moved back to the United States in 1988, and I proceeded to start Kindergarten in Newport News, Va., where I'd spend my middle school and high school years. This would be home for the rest of my life, but this was also where I learned how tough my parents really were.

Now, my pops is old-school—he made sure a roof was over your head and there was food on the table. Everyone who meets him likes him, but he's definitely a straight shooter. He's not going to bullshit you, and when he speaks, people listen.

But I'm not going to lie—having a father in the Army can be tough. When my parents moved to Virginia, my dad was stationed at Fort Eustis, in Newport News, Va. Soon after we moved there, he was deployed to Egypt, and with my parents' determination to make a steady home for me and Alexon, that meant mom—who worked at ATSC (Army Training Support Center) on Fort Eustis—was left to take care of us alone.

That was definitely tough on all of us. At least nowadays, when a man is away from his family, he can FaceTime. But back then, there was none of that—only phone calls. Now that I'm a father, I can say that I know that had to be tough on my dad, but he was doing what he needed to do for the betterment of the family, a sacrifice I appreciate even more now that I'm older.

Still, Pops was definitely missed around the house. And by 1992, with my brother in high school—he was always off doing his own thing, whether it was playing sports or hanging out with his friends—and me in third grade, my dad's absence only led to my mom and I becoming closer.

Let me tell you this, too: when I was a child, Mom Dukes—that's what I call her—was a superwoman. She cooked, she cleaned, she worked 9 to 5. There was no nanny, nobody coming in helping her. She was old school in her own way, just like my dad; she was about going to work, cooking, and cleaning, all while finding time to help me with my home-work and take me to all my extracurricular activities.

Little did we know at the time that things were going to get much more complicated for us all.

*"I wish I could take the pain away, if you can make it through the
night, there's a brighter day"*
Tupac, *Dear Mama*

I'll never forget the day I first started worrying about my mom's health.
It was October of 1992, and we lived in an apartment on the Army base
in Newport News. I remember my mom was dyeing her hair one day, and
her face started to swell up. I didn't know much about anything at the
time, but I knew something wasn't right. I guess she could tell, because
she preemptively started calming me down.

"It's okay, 'Toine," she told me. "I'll be alright."

And initially, we thought she was. The doctors checked her out and
said there was nothing wrong with her, she was just having an allergic
reaction to the hair dye. We were all relieved at first, but after a few more
days of her not feeling normal—something was just off, she said—she
went back to the hospital and they ran some more tests.

Turns out she had a tumor at the base of her brain.

Now, you know how parents are. This was a scary surgery, but mom
and dad tried to keep me and Alexon from worrying, so they never really
said "Hey, this is what's going on." But leading up to the surgery, she was
in and out of the hospital, prepping for it. At the time, I had a close
friend by the name of Jermaine that stayed behind us and from time to
time. I would stay with his family when my mom was in the hospital.

I'll be honest, I don't remember much else leading up to her surgery.
All I knew was that Mom was going to have surgery, and that she had
checked into the hospital a few days prior, just so the doctors could see
how she would react to the medicine they were gonna put her on. Still,
we visited her the day before the surgery, and that night, I was nervous.
I really didn't get good sleep due to the fact we were unsure of what the
outcome would be.

My mom had the surgery in the early morning, and while my dad
stayed at the hospital with her—he promised he'd call with an update—
I just stayed in the house with Lex, playing video games like "Sonic the

Hedgehog" and "Mortal Kombat" until my dad finally called around 4 p.m., nearly 14 hours after her surgery had begun.

"Mom's out of surgery, she's doing fine," he said, clearly relieved. "She's in the recovery room. I'll be on my way to get you guys pretty soon."

By the time my dad swung by and scooped us up in his Isuzu Rodeo, I was relieved, too. When we got there, I tried to keep my cool as we sat in the waiting room, but there was no way I was ready to see what my mom looked like after the surgery. Her face was swollen, and the big white bandages wrapped around her head ... my mom was a strong woman—she was actually the disciplinarian, the one who whooped us when we messed up—and I'd never seen her like that before. It was just too much for eight-year-old 'Toine, and I started crying.

After the doctor suggested they take me out of the room, my dad did just that. My dad was a tough dude, but he wasn't mad at me for crying or anything. He knew how close he'd come to losing his wife, how close we'd come to losing our mother. Relieved that God had smiled down on us, he simply hugged me.

It was not the last time my mom would face a serious medical issue, it turns out. Hell, it wasn't even the last time I'd see a family member face death during my adolescence.

While my mom eventually made a full recovery—and man, she was back on her feet in about a month or so, working and running the house and taking care of me and everything—I'd soon learn even more about the fragility of life, thanks to two more scary situations I witnessed family members endure over the next 24 months.

Ring! Ring! Ring!

Some of us didn't even hear the phone ring on this summer evening in 1993. My parents had taken me and Lex on a family vacation to my parents' hometown of Lake View, South Carolina, and while the phone was ringing at my aunt's house, many of us were in the living room, laughing and playing Pitty Pat, a card game that always got the juices flowing amongst the family.

So much so that, even when my aunt answered the phone and—in an unusual tone—told my dad that someone wanted to speak to him, none of us even picked up on it.

"Uh huh," Dad said, phone to his ear. "What?!"

Dad hung up the phone and sprinted toward the door. Mom followed, and the rest of us did, too, following him to the Isuzu Rodeo as we piled in. I was sitting in the third row, wondering what the hell was going on. He didn't explain anything, but I knew something was wrong from the look on his face.

As dad flew down the street, a left here, a right there, you could see the swirling red and blue police lights well into the distance before we arrived at the destination, a house on the left I'd never seen before. Dad peeled off to the right side of the road and barely came to a stop before he jumped out and ran inside the house where police and paramedics were standing outside.

A minute later, my dad emerged from the house with tears in his eyes. This was unusual because I'd never seen my dad cry—even when my mom was going through her situation with the brain tumor—so we knew something had to be terribly wrong.

"Eddie's dead," he told her, voice shaking. "He's gone!"

Inside, I felt that familiar mixture of confusion and fear rise from the pit of my stomach, the same combination that caused me to break down next to my mother's hospital bed after her surgery. But weirdly enough, I did not cry at this time. I'm not sure why, but trust me—hearing my dad say that hit me like a Mack truck.

See, Eddie was my dad's oldest brother. He was the life of the party. Some of the stories my mom and dad tell about him to this day, I could only imagine some of things we could've gotten into. He was a wild child, someone who lived on the edge. But to me, he was just Uncle Eddie, the tall, fun-loving guy who used to playfully drag me through my grandmother's house by my feet and beat me up. Uncle Eddie also had a huge afro and a big smile. I loved Unc.

So, over the next five minutes—as my dad came to grips with reality—we all just sat there like, is this real? We'd just seen him the day before. And personally, I'm thinking not *my* uncle—he can't be dead.

But he was, and to this day, no one knows what exactly happened. The police think it was a possible murder-suicide, though, with my uncle being a victim. He was lying on the floor with a woman and a man, and I remember my parents saying it's possible the dude killed my uncle, the woman, and then himself. But again, no one knows for sure.

All I know is that after that horrible night, my dad—who never stopped mourning the senseless loss of one of his two older brothers—always reminded me and Lex to have each other's backs, and to maintain our deep bond.

"You guys are brothers," he'd tell us. "You'd better be there for each other because you never know what life will throw at you, and most of the time, the best friend you'll ever have is your sibling."

People say that siblings who have a large age gap, like me and my brother, often aren't as close as those who, say, go to middle school and high school together. But that wasn't really the case with me and Lex. Even then, I could never imagine the pain of losing him.

In retrospect, I can't believe that my brother, who was 17 at the time, would soon put that to the test about a year later.

In the fall of 1994, Alexon went off to college at Delaware State, basically leaving me and Mom Dukes on base. She'd gotten back to 100 percent—she was back to working on the base and everything—and with my dad back to Egypt, it was just us for a while.

Even though I missed my brother, I was proud of him for going to college. When he went, I knew it was something I wanted to do, too, since I saw it was possible.

I was a pretty good student and my attendance was good, too. I knew that I better be, because if I came home with D's and F's, there would have been a belt or shoes upside my butt. Besides, I loved playing sports—I played football, baseball, and basketball at the time—and my parents stressed that if I wanted to play sports, I needed to make sure my grades were good.

Lex, like me, loved football. At 6-foot-2, he was a pretty good player in his day, and even though he didn't earn any scholarships out of high school, he was thinking seriously about walking on at Delaware State in the spring. He'd never get the chance, though.

Around Thanksgiving of 1994, just a few months into his first year on campus, I remember being at home with my parents when the phone rang late at night. I was excited that night, because I'd just finished my third year of organized football, and my team was having a banquet the next day. By that point, I turned into a pretty good running back, scoring three or four touchdowns a game, but my dreams of the football recognition that was to come the next day were soon interrupted once my mother answered the phone that night around 1 a.m.

"Mrs. Bethea," one of my brother's friends told her. "Lex has been shot."

"Say what?" she said, annoyed. "Stop playing on my phone."

Now, my mom originally thought it was a joke because Lex and his friends always played jokes on her, telling her Lex is in trouble or hurt or in jail whenever they called. They knew how much she cared, and it became a sort of understood joke.

But not this time.

"Naw, for real, Mrs. Bethea," he said. "Lex has been shot."

So after dealing with her tumor, and watching her husband deal with the murder of his brother, my mom is thinking the worst. She wakes me out of my sleep, wakes my dad up and we rush to get dressed and get to the hospital.

At this point, we're in the Isuzu Rodeo. I'm half-sleep, and they aren't telling me anything. But my dad must have been having flashbacks of what happened with my uncle, because he was so disoriented, he drove us to Mary Immaculate Hospital instead of the Riverside Regional Medical Center, where Lex was.

Understand, my dad's specialty in the military was transportation, so he was keen on knowing where to go. So seeing him go to the wrong place let me know that this shit was serious.

We eventually drove the 20 minutes to Riverside, where we were taken to a small, dark waiting room with four chairs and a lamp. That's when a hospital chaplain entered through the door and started asking us questions.

"Is your son a black male?"

"Yes."

"Over six-feet tall?"

"Yes."

The chaplain's face was blank.

"He didn't make it."

I looked at my parents' faces, and saw a mixture of shock, sadness, anger—the whole spectrum. My mom started to cry, and I felt that oh-so-familiar mixture of confusion and fear rise to the surface.

"Are you sure?" my dad asked. "You must have the wrong person!"

He was sure, he said. And right at the point where I might have started to cry at the thought of losing my only brother, a doctor walked in the room.

"Is your son's name Alexon Bethea?" he asked.

"Yeah! Yeah! Yeah!" my mom yelled.

"Well, there's been a mistake. Your son is actually about to go into surgery right now."

Talk about relief! But there was also anger, because how can a hospital get something like that wrong? For about 60 seconds, we thought he was gone. My parents were pissed, and rightfully so. Like, what type of motherfuckers do shit like that? You've got to have the right information before you tell somebody their son didn't make it!

Turns out, Lex's injuries were serious—getting shot is more than a notion, okay?—but they weren't going to be life threatening. His surgery to remove the bullets took a couple of hours, and after he was moved to the recovery room, we were able to go back and see him.

Lex was able to talk, but he'd been given some meds to handle the pain and was slurring his words. He laid on the bed, eyes half open, and connected to a catheter. It wasn't until several hours later that we got the full story from him about what happened.

Lex and his friends were leaving a roller-skating rink when they saw a couple of guys standing outside the entrance. They started walking toward their car when suddenly, they heard shots ringing out. Obviously, Lex's first reaction was to flee, so he ran across the street to the U-Haul store, where there were a bunch of U-Haul trucks in the parking lot. He figured he'd hide there until the shooting stopped.

Problem was, whoever it was those guys were shooting at had the same idea, because the longer Lex waited behind the trucks, the louder the shots got. While ducking, he saw bullets hitting the ground around him, and when he peeked around the trucks, he saw some guys in a car shooting in his direction. Then he looked underneath the truck and saw guys, on foot, shooting toward the car.

So at this point, he's caught in the crossfire, and didn't know what to do. His first instinct was to get up and run until he wasn't in the crossfire. But his adrenaline must have been pumping like crazy or something, because when he finally circled back with his friends in front of the skating rink, somebody pointed out to him that his shirt and pants were full of holes, soaked in dark red blood, in fact. Shortly after that, he passed out on a table inside of the skating rink and was taken to the hospital.

Lex had been grazed on the eyebrow with a bullet, and he was also shot in the leg in his main artery—roughly the same place where Washington Redskins safety Sean Taylor was struck with a bullet in 2007. Taylor ended up dying, but the bullet went through my brother's leg and Lex ended up making a full recovery.

One of Lex's friends had been shot as well, and so was a female he didn't know, and they ended up being okay, but one dude actually died in the shootout.

That was a reminder of how blessed we were that Lex was okay, though I'd soon realize how much three family members' brushes with death—in three consecutive years, during my formative years, no less—would come to shape my personality down the road.

Looking back, I'm sure that Lex's near-death experience reinforced to me how life can be taken from you in an instant. This was my brother, and he was 7 ½ years older than me, but had things gone a different way, he would no longer be on this earth.

What it all taught me was that there is absolutely no time to live in fear or doubt—if you want something in life, you better go get it. We are all given one life and we must find our purpose, but you can only do that by subduing fear and living our lives to our greatest potential. I wasn't completely conscious of all this at the time, but those experiences instilled two things in me: a sense of gratitude for every single day, and an urgency about living life to the fullest. Both have served me well throughout my life.

By the age of 12, all the shit I'd witnessed taught me that there's a lot of things going on in this world, and you better pay attention to your surroundings.

This was a lesson that would benefit me in sixth grade, when my parents moved us off the base at Fort Eustis into a house in Newport News, Virginia, which was 10-15 minutes away. You've probably heard of Newport News before. It's a part of the Hampton Roads region, an area that has produced a lot of great athletes, including Hall of Famer Allen Iverson, Michael Vick, and lots of others. I could go on and on.

I grew up in uptown Newport News, and I always say that where we were from, you get a lil' bit of everything. You had your middle class families that went to work every day, but you also had your areas where you definitely had to be aware of your surroundings. Some of my class-mates that I went to school with were murdered, and others ended up doing jail time. In 2007, one of my good friends from my childhood got caught up in the drug game and was shot in the head in the backseat of a car, right around the corner from his mom and dad's house.

So, growing up, there were a lot of times when you could've easily gone down the wrong path, literally. And while a lot of shit was going on, it was important for you to be aware of your surroundings. If you're in a place and somebody walks in and you see what type of aura and energy that person brings, your antennas go up. There's been a number of times where I went to a party, heard a couple people talking about shit I wasn't cool with and me and my homeboys decided to bounce. Some people, they don't have to worry about that because of the environment they grow up in. But in Newport News, I certainly did.

And considering trouble had found my brother—when he was away at college, no less—my parents were intent on keeping me too busy to get in trouble. Not that I needed much help staying active. By the time I was in junior high, I was doing a lot, playing organized football and basketball. I'd quit baseball by that point because I got hit with one too many balls—those boys were throwing some heat and I was like "Naw, this ain't for me"—but I was always on the go, playing sports somewhere.

My parents like to say I was a restless kid—they joke that I had a hard time sitting still and, in retrospect, I don't think this was a coincidence. I think all the crazy shit that happened to my family by then taught me the importance of never taking life for granted and always having some sense of urgency about you. I mean, my Uncle Eddie was dead, my brother ran through some bullets, and my mom beat a brain tumor. That's a lot to happen to somebody before age 11.

After all that, I think I subconsciously realized that if there were some things I wanted to accomplish, then I'd better get my ass out there and do them, because tomorrow isn't promised. I know it's a cliché, but it's true. I mean, my brother had thought about walking on to Delaware State's football team, for example, but a freak tragedy had taken that from him. Life is crazy like that.

That said, I'm proud of Lex. Because while he understandably wasn't comfortable being at Delaware State anymore, he still went back to school after getting shot. He ended up transferring to Old Dominion University, which was four hours south of Delaware State but only 40 minutes away from Newport News.

This, of course, thrilled me, because that meant I was able to see my big brother more. He even let me hang out with him in college some weekends, as he'd come pick me up and bring me to his dorm. At the time, I was really into basketball, so I'd be down at Old Dominion, playing open gym hoops with them, and even though it was a little thing, it was something that was special to me.

All this, I think, led to me realizing that I definitely wanted to go to college. They just seemed to be having so much fun, and besides, when you have a big brother, you always want to follow in his footsteps, and there was absolutely no doubt I looked up to Lex. He's the reason I was so into sports, in fact, because he loved to play football and basketball, and when I was a kid, I just wanted to do what my big brother did. So I tagged along whenever I could, even for our brutally-physical street-ball games with the older kids. Those experiences are why—long before the NFL was ever on my mind—basketball was actually my first love, and why I dreamed of being a star basketball player at the University of North Carolina.

My brother eventually ended up leaving Old Dominion to get a regular job—he—s happy now, working at a shipyard with a son and a fiancé—but honestly, he had already done his part to set me on a course to go to college, simply by showing me what university life was like at such a formative age.

Add that to my parents' influence—remember, they didn't mess around—and the brushes with death my three family members experienced, and, hell, I probably had rule No. 1 down before I even got to junior high. I definitely had all the urgency and motivation I needed to pursue my dream of earning a college scholarship and make it come true.

Life, of course, is not a fairy tale. I'd learn that when I got to high school, when—despite my exploits on the football field and basketball court—I started to realize that making my dream a reality would be far easier said than done, even though looking back at it, I wouldn't change a thing.

All the crazy things that happened to me over the next several chapters taught me that my life is bigger than me; all those experiences were given to me to help someone else. I believe that good people inspire themselves, but great people inspire others. Just like I hope you take something from this book, I hope you know that someone is waiting for your gift, your story, your experience, and they are waiting for you to live so that they can, in turn, live, too.

Bet on Yourself

THE VARSITY BASKETBALL COACH WALKED into the cramped locker room, eyes ablaze. We'd just lost another game, and he was looking for something—specifically someone, I'd soon find out.

This was the winter of my senior year at Denbigh High School, and I was a two-year starter at point guard, not to mention a team captain. By then, I'd devoted a lot of my energy to basketball, but I was only about 5 foot 10, and one of my high school football coaches—Tracy Harrod, who'd played college football at James Madison back in his day—had already pulled me aside in the hallway one day my junior year and given me the real.

"'Toine, I don't know too many 5'10" NBA stars," he told me, with a shrug. "I know you love basketball, but this football thing can save you and your parents a lot of money for college."

I begrudgingly realized he was right. I had to keep it funky (real) with myself, especially when I only grew about an inch after that. Playing for the University of North Carolina's basketball team was definitely not in my future.

Still, though, I was an OK basketball player, a Rajon Rondo-type who got everybody shots and scored enough—maybe 10 or 12 points a game—to keep defenses honest. I'd gotten a few small-school looks for hoops—Fayetteville State University, for example—but I figured if I was going to play sports in college, I might as well play one where my height wouldn't be such a massive detriment to going pro.

As a high school player, though, my height mattered less. We weren't great my senior year, but I'd like to think I earned my teammates' respect by doing things the right way and leading from the front. I never missed a practice, I was never late, and I always tried to do what I was told.

But you never would have known that, based on the way our varsity coach—Jerry Farrior—decided to come at me one night after a loss. For the first time in my life, I actually decided to quit something, and in the process, ended up stumbling across my second rule to overcoming the odds. Looking back at it, I still don't believe what I did was right, but it was definitely a situation I learned from.

Coach Farrior set his gaze upon us and started in on us. I was always the type of person who could take hard coaching—all of my coaches growing up were hard on us, and they had to be, given how tough some of us were—but after three minutes of this guy starting every sentence with "'Toine, 'Toine, 'Toine," my simmering anger finally exploded to the surface. I was already pissed we lost the game; I wasn't about to be the scapegoat, not after the example I set on a daily basis.

"Fuck this!" I yelled. "Y'all can have this shit! I'm not gonna come out here and bust my ass every practice and in every game, be the leader of the team, do whatever's asked for me, and keep getting ripped!"

Now, when you are the leader of anything—a team, a department at your job, anything—a lot of things tend to fall on your shoulders, even if it isn't your fault. After all, the saying "to whom much is given, much will be required," is real.

But while I knew that at the time—and my parents raised me to be respectful of authority (my brother and I still say "yes, sir" and "no, sir" to our elders, to this day)—right is right and wrong is wrong, and Coach Farrior, who had been riding me all season, had gone too far.

I wasn't done yelling.

"If I did something, you tell me what I did wrong. But you can't just put this whole game on me!"

And with that, I ripped off my jersey, threw it against a locker, put on my clothes and stormed out. I must have been walking really fast as I made my way to the car, because as I passed through the gym, I noticed people staring at me.

"Man, what the fuck is going on?" I heard someone say.

I finally got to the car, unlocked it, and dropped into the passenger seat, waiting for my mom—who came to all my games—to join me. When she did, she looked confused.

"What's up?" she asked.

I was so angry I didn't even try to censor myself.

"Ma, I'm not dealing with this shit anymore," I said angrily. "Every motherfucking thing he was saying was 'Toine 'Toine 'Toine 'Toine."

"I understand," she said.

"I'm quitting," I told her.

My parents hated quitters—they never let me quit any sport or any activity in the middle—so I knew I was really reaching on that. But that's how pissed I was.

"You know you can't quit," she told me. "You have to talk to your dad, first, and you already know what he's gonna say."

"Ya'll can talk to whoever, I'm not gonna do this shit."

That was one of the first times I ever really defied my parents. I was about to turn 18 that following July, and that was how strongly I felt I'd been wronged.

As I sat in the car, a bunch of people who'd seen me storm out kept glancing at me. A few even came to the car to find out what was going on. I didn't tell them, though; as pissed as I was, I still saw it as a team matter, and I didn't think it was anyone else's business.

But when one of Coach Farrior's assistant coaches came to the car and asked me what was up, I basically unleashed.

"Man, you heard that shit in there," I yelled. "Watch the game! You know what I do for this team. Yo, I'm done with this shit, Coach."

And if you're thinking "Toine, you were overreacting," well, guess what—that coach didn't. He understood my point, and he also knew how competitive I was.

"You'll look back on this and regret it," he said, cautiously.

"Yeah, I get it," I responded. "Well, I'm just gonna regret it. I'm not gonna deal with that shit no more."

Now, the awkward thing about this situation was that Coach Farrior was my fifth-period teacher my senior year. So, I knew I'd have to see him the next day. I went to his class and didn't say anything for 40 minutes, then I skipped practice. That's when he knew I was serious. I went to talk to him after class the next day, before practice, and we tried to hash it out.

"Sometimes, after a loss, you say things the wrong way," he explained. "You're the leader of the team. I expect you to lead the team and be the coach on the floor."

And really, the way he explained it that day was the way he should have explained things after the game. But I was still heated.

"Yo, Coach, I been doing that—I've been doing that the whole time," I said. "I just feel like you blamed me for everything."

"Nah, I wasn't trying to do that."

"But that's what you did."

"I apologize for that," he said. "I wasn't trying to do that. I was just trying to point out some things you did wrong."

When Coach Farrior apologized, I'm not gonna lie, I felt vindicated. I thought the things I was doing on the court for the team were right, and in that moment, I saw the benefit of always making good choices. When you do the right things, you know you've got the truth on your side, and you can always call bullshit. If you never miss a practice, if you're never late, if you always work hard, always play hard ... that gives you the confidence to know you put in the necessary work to make things go your way.

We continued to talk, and eventually, we squared it away. I returned to the team, and I never missed another practice. We still didn't have a great season, but I ended up making second-team all-district in basketball.

My high school football career, however, was certainly a little more decorated. A few months earlier, I'd just wrapped up my final season at

Denbigh, when I was all-district and all-region in my second year as a starter in the highest high school classification in Virginia. I even made the Virginia High School Coaches Association's all-star game.

Now, in retrospect, I'm sure you're saying to yourself—of course you did, 'Toine! You played 13 years in the NFL. Why wouldn't football be your meal ticket dating back to high school?

There were just two problems with that line of thinking. The first problem was that I was a 5-foot-11, 170-pound middle linebacker as a senior. And the second problem—which was not unrelated—was that none of the big college programs in the area thought I was good enough to offer a scholarship.

Beating those odds to make my dream of playing D-1 football come true would not only require an unwavering belief in myself—one fortified by my experience with Coach Farrior—it would also require a little bit of luck.

By the time National Signing Day—the day high school football players from all over the country officially sign scholarship papers to attend the school of their choice—rolled around in February 2002, I had zero Division I offers and nothing to sign. It was just another day for me at school.

The same can't be said for many nearby players my age group, though. That year, Michael Vick's little brother, Marcus, was the No. 8 player in the country, according to Rivals. He went to Virginia Tech, while Princess Anne defensive end Kai Parham (the No. 11 player in the country) and Heritage running back Michael Johnson (No. 14) went to Virginia.

All three of those guys played high school ball within 30 minutes of me, and so did a handful of other guys from my district who were seniors like me, including Warwick receiver Brenden Hill and Bethel corner-back Jimmy Williams, who both went to Virginia Tech. But while the media was making a big deal about those guys on Signing Day, I wasn't even listed on Rivals, let alone ranked.

Let me be clear, though: I wasn't jealous of those guys. I was actually happy for them. Hampton Roads is a tough place, and I salute any high schooler who gets out of there to go to college to make a better life for themselves. There were a lot of traps out there, and I saw many people who came into ninth grade with me who weren't there in 11th or 12th grade because they'd dropped out or gotten in trouble.

So, yes, I've never been one to hate on another man's accomplishment, even though I certainly felt like I was being overlooked. I remained hopeful I'd get an opportunity to play D-1 ball, but by then, things were looking dim. A few months earlier, right before basketball season, I'd visited a couple of local schools, Christopher Newport University and Randolph-Macon, who were interested in me. But those were Division 3 schools, which don't even award scholarships. They were talking about giving me some partial financial aid, but it wouldn't have been the full ride I craved. A few other schools, like Fayetteville State, Bridgewater University, and Norfolk State, sniffed around, but I never got an offer.

However, I'd soon get a break that I couldn't predict, as Coach Petty was named Howard University's head coach on January 26, 2002. Like Norfolk State, Howard was a historically black college in Division 1-AA, which was a pretty competitive level of football, especially when compared to Division 3. They played in the Mid-Eastern Athletic Conference along with several other HBCUs, and since it was located in Washington, D.C., it was only a three-hour drive away from home, which made it far enough to spread my wings, but close enough to keep my mom from going crazy.

I hadn't heard from them at all before Coach Petty was hired. But he already knew me from his Norfolk State days, and when he hired one of his good friends, A.C. Cauthorn—who happened to be my high school's head football coach—it gave me an additional in, as Coach Cauthorn persuaded him to bring me in for a visit.

I got there on a warm Friday in early March and, man, I immediately saw why alumni call Howard "The Mecca." There were so many young black men and women out there, chilling on "The Yard," the large, tree-heavy, grassy space in the middle of campus, surrounded by historic buildings named after some of our most memorable alumni.

But while The Yard was just a cool spot in general, it was the people who made it special. Everywhere you looked, there were beautiful black people, all very unique. Ladies of all shapes, sizes, and colors were dressed to the hilt—designer fashions, stilettos and all. You had the fraternities and sororities stepping, the actors and dancers putting on a full show on the steps of the Fine Arts building, the business students hurrying across the yard in suits ... with a ton of students just laughing and joking and having a blast. Even now, I get chills thinking about it.

"Yo," I remember telling my host on the visit. "Is this everyday life here?"

And it was! That night, we went to the La-Tex party (a popular party thrown by students from Louisiana and Texas) and my head was spinning. The music was on point, the girls were fine, and the football players on the team were cool. I thought the four years in high school, just running around with my homeboys was fun, but now, here I was hanging out with these dudes I'd never met before, having the time of my life.

The next day, we went to an afternoon basketball game at Burr Gymnasium, where Howard's men's basketball team played on campus. Ironically enough, they were playing Norfolk State—the school that was interested in me but never offered—and they had these seats sectioned off for us. I remember looking around at the band, which played with so much soul, and the cheerleaders, who danced with so much spirit, and thinking: So this is what "A Different World"—the popular early-90s television show—was talking about! And I'm in it.

Later that night, I remember going back to my hotel room—they put us up in the Ritz-Carlton—and telling my parents that I wanted to go to Howard. I just knew it was the type of culture I could thrive in. Everybody was upbeat, there was no drama or fighting, and the players on the team were family-oriented. Hell, our hosts on the trip treated me and the other recruits like we'd already been there for a year.

There was just one little problem—Coach Petty had explained before the trip that they were basically out of scholarships, so they couldn't offer a full ride. And if I'm being honest, what they could offer in financial relief barely amounted to a partial scholarship. But my dad wasn't worried.

"You'll still be able to go to school for four years, and you'll still play football, even if you didn't get recruited," dad said. "Just work and control what you can control, which is what?"

"My work ethic and my grades," I said.

"That's right," he said.

My dad was giving me the benefit of the doubt when he said I'd be able to play football at Howard for four years, though. Coach Petty didn't promise me anything beyond the first year—all he said is that they would give me a scholarship if I earned one. If I didn't, I knew that meant I'd likely transfer to a smaller school, since I was so set on playing football.

That said, I didn't think about the worst-case scenario much, or how I could have potentially spared myself some trouble by just going to Randolph-Macon or Christopher Newport off the bat. My parents believed in me, and I wanted to believe it would work out, especially after that killer recruiting weekend.

At the end of the day, Howard wasn't exactly the opportunity I dreamed of—it wasn't Division 1, and it certainly wasn't North Carolina hoops. But it was an opportunity, nonetheless, and by then, I was especially comfortable betting on myself. I knew I'd make good choices and do the right things, which would put me on firm ground when it came to getting what I wanted.

I signed the financial aid agreement before I left town that Sunday, knowing that the stakes for believing in myself were much higher now than simply winning an argument with a coach. My future hung in the balance.

By the time I arrived on Howard's campus in the summer of 2002, I had a chip on my shoulder the size of Virginia. I'd been working my ass off for weeks, running hills and lifting for weeks, because walk-ons like me didn't have the luxury of reporting out of shape—not if I was serious about proving all those schools that didn't bother to recruit me wrong.

The first proving ground at Howard would be summer conditioning drills, where freshmen learn what college ball was all about. The players are bigger, stronger, and faster, and, like most freshmen, I was a little uneasy and had no idea what to expect.

I had reason to be nervous, it turns out.

For our very first conditioning test, we all were tasked with running two miles in under 12 minutes at the crack of dawn. We were told that if you didn't make your times, you had to run it again. I thought I was in pretty good shape at the time, and I ended up making my eight laps … until my new defensive backs coach, Ron Bolton, said I had only done seven laps in the allotted time and thus, had to get up the next morning and run that shit again.

When I tell you I was hot, man … wooo, I was fuming. Because to me, he made it look like I'd failed the conditioning test and I wasn't prepared, when actually, I had been practicing. What would Coach Petty and Coach Cauthorn think after they brought me in at the last minute? I've always been a guy that could work out on my own and get the job done. It was so unfair.

I went back and forth with Coach Bolton about it, because, frankly, I didn't want to have to get up and run those miles again the next morning. Unfortunately, I lost that argument, and it wouldn't be the last time I lost an argument to Coach. But I will say this: the next day, I made my time again, and I was sure Coach Bolton—a man who would eventually play a major role in getting me to the NFL—got it right.

In retrospect, the fact that Coach Bolton introduced me to a little adversity early on was fitting, since Howard's football program was—like me, ironically—constantly trying to do more with less, as the funding for athletic programs for HBCUs isn't great, especially when compared to the big state schools you see every Saturday on ESPN and ABC. When I hear the guys I play with in the NFL talk about how great they had it in college, I straight up tell them that I don't know if they would have made it at Howard, because we didn't have *half* of what they had.

At Howard, for instance, we didn't have the meal table of some of these bigger schools, like an Alabama or a Louisiana State. We didn't even have a nutritionist—for us, eating healthy meant going to Subway. We mainly ate in the cafeteria—or simply the "Café," as we students called it—and when that was closed at night, we'd eat fast food from Domino's and or a little Chinese place behind Cook Hall, our athletic dorm, called Howard China or "HoChi," as we called it.

HoChi is legendary among Howard students for its really cheap food that always hit the spot. It is open all night and it's located only a block away from the freshmen and athletic dorms. When we were hungry, we'd take whatever little money we could scrounge together and make that short walk—sometimes through a dark alley because it was a little quicker—to get the wings and fries with mumbo sauce, a really addictive sweet-and-sour condiment you can only find in D.C.

Just imagine a tiny, worn building on the corner with an interior to match, complete with the workers taking your order behind a bullet-proof glass. But the food was so good, so cheap, and so close—the closest grocery store was a 10-minute drive away, and many of us didn't have cars—we regularly patronized the place, even though we heard about Howard students occasionally getting robbed by locals who lived in the neighborhood. You won't find a member of the Howard team back then that didn't eat there regularly.

When we weren't eating at HoChi or practicing at Greene Stadium, our home football field (Howard didn't have a practice field, mind you), we were often working out in our modest weight room, which was located in the basement of one of our dormitories. There were exposed pipes in the ceiling, and it was the size of a large three-bedroom apartment, maybe 1,500 square feet. It was dimly-lit, and was comprised of about five bench and squat platforms on one side, with a dumbbell rack and five machines on the other.

Still, when I walked in there the first time, it didn't strike me as inadequate, even though I now know there are some high school gyms that are better than Howard's. At the time, it was better than what I had at my high school, so it was an upgrade. I'm grateful that I didn't know any better, in retrospect; that made it easier for me to take weight training seriously, since I wasn't jaded by the facilities or anything.

Fortunately, what Howard lacked in facilities and nutrition, it more than made up for in coaching. Despite my rough start with Coach Bolton, I'd eventually come to realize this sometimes-abrasive man was the best position coach I'd ever had—including my 13-plus years in the NFL.

"I don't say a word-I don't say a word-was on my grind and
I got what I deserve"
Meek Mill, *Dreams and Nightmares*

Prior to enrolling at Howard, I had never backpedaled in a game before—remember, in high school I was an outside linebacker as a junior and my senior year I played middle linebacker, which are both positions that require you to play downhill.

But playing safety in college? Yeah, I'd have get comfortable backpedaling, and soon. I'd also have to train my eyes from a different vantage point if I wanted to get on the field fast enough to avoid redshirt year, which I didn't have time for. I was trying to prove I belonged so I can earn a scholarship.

All that said—and this is truly remarkable—I never felt like I was behind. Ever. And I'd have to credit Coach Bolton for that. He was teaching me stuff during my freshman and sophomore years that coaches in the NFL were teaching the pros. I was eager for knowledge, and I picked it up quick. Eventually, I endearingly started calling him "old man," because I genuinely respected his knowledge—he had played in the NFL for 11 years—and I always listened to him. Plus, he was a quasi-local cat, like me, as his hometown of Petersburg, Va., was only 90 minutes away from Newport News.

Coach Bolton definitely had a gruff side, though, and as players, it strangely made us like him more. He had an edge to him, and we liked it. He'd even curse us out on the field at practice sometimes. In time, me and the rest of the defensive backs began to imitate his favorite line, which was a sarcastic-but-funny "you sorry motherfucker!" after someone messed up on the field.

But really, it was all love, and we know that, because when we got in the meeting room, he was totally different. He really cared for us, and there were many moments where me and my fellow defensive backs would just sit back and talk about how we knew he coached us hard but he only wanted us to get better.

Now truthfully, I love the guy because he was the first one on the coaching staff to really, really believe that I could play. I sat and watched for most of my freshman year, but toward the end of the season, he straight up told me he was going to get me a few snaps at safety, and after that, he kept telling Keith Gilmore, our defensive coordinator at the time, that I can play until I actually did start getting in games toward the end of the year.

By the end of my freshman season, I was about 185 pounds, after reporting at 175 pounds just five months before. The NFL wasn't even a thought—I was way too focused on just earning a full ride. But I'm not going to lie, it did enter my consciousness in May 2003—the spring before my sophomore year—when I saw our best offensive lineman, Marques Ogden, get drafted in the sixth round and by the Jacksonville Jaguars and our best linebacker, Tracy White, get picked up by the Green Bay Packers as an undrafted free agent that same year.

To be able to watch Marques and Tracy play my freshman year and see them get those looks, that's when it kind of clicked, like hey, it is a possibility. In 2003, another player who went to an HBCU—Rashean Mathis of Bethune-Cookman—actually got selected in the second round by Jacksonville, and I realized that getting drafted was a possibility coming from the MEAC. But again, my goal wasn't to play in the NFL; all I was trying to do was prove to Coach Petty that I deserved a full scholarship.

That would come soon enough, though. The summer before my sophomore year, I was invited back to Howard for the second session of summer school after spending the first session back home in Newport News. I was pretty optimistic I'd be put on full scholarship because Coach Petty gave me money to come back for the second session of summer school, and I knew that was typically a good sign. But I'd received no official assurances, and they kind of left me in the dark during that first summer school session when I was at home.

That's why I'll never forget the day Coach Petty called me into the office that summer and told me I was getting a full ride for my sophomore season. I went into his office, and there the scholarship packet was.

"You did everything we asked you to do," he said. "And like I told you I would, if you did that, I was going to give you your money entering your sophomore year."

I signed it immediately. I couldn't wait to call home.

"You ain't gotta pay that money no more," I yelled to my parents.

Mom and Dad were excited, I was excited—it was a good day for the family. That's the dream, growing up, that's what you want—being able to go to school, play football, and get a degree for free.

Yet, even though I was finally a full scholarship player entering my sophomore year, it was easy for me to keep the chip on my shoulder, even after after I grew into a surprise starter the next year and a potential NFL draft prospect as a senior.

To me, the way it played out was validation that while you might not get the position of your dreams at first—and most of the time, it's because someone might not want to invest in you right away—you can't wait for someone to put you on, or help you out. Yeah, Howard gave me a chance. But I had to take that chance and run with it, and I had to bet on myself to make it happen.

You have to believe in yourself so much that it becomes contagious, so much so that others begin to believe in you, as well. People may not see the vision until you show them through action, so do the work, trust the process, and know that the reward will follow suit! Don't limit your challenges! Instead, challenge your limits.

But here's the thing: just know that once you've prevailed over an obstacle, life is still just a series of challenges. When you break down one barrier, another one will emerge in your path. That's what happened to me once I shifted my goals from simply earning a scholarship and a starting job to becoming an NFL player, as I was forced to deal with the biggest gut-punches of my young life—back-to-back, no less—if I wanted to become only the sixth Howard player to ever be selected in the NFL Draft.

You see, the slights never stop coming when you're an underdog, but you can't use that as an excuse. You may not get the same start as others—underdogs never do—but whatever hand you're dealt, you've got to play the hell out of it and know that you and you alone are enough.

How I dealt with the draft process, I think, proves that the philosophy works.

Take Slights Personally

"The motivation for me is them telling me what I could not be."
Pharrell Williams, *So Ambitious*

MY SENIOR YEAR AT HOWARD, we played Bethune-Cookman at Greene Stadium, and trust me, it was one of those games you'd rather forget. We got blown out 45-16, dropping our record to 4-6, and let's just say it wasn't one of my best games.

Bethune-Cookman ran a triple option, and while I'd played great against them the year before in Daytona, this time, they were sending two people at me, trying to cut me, and I just missed way too many tackles. That was uncharacteristic of me, because I prided myself on being a really confident, really good tackler. I took horrible angles to the ball that day. I'm telling you, I might have finished with a lot of tackles that day, but if you looked at this film, you'd say to yourself, "This isn't like 'Toine," and I knew it right then and there.

I put the game behind me quickly, though, or at least I thought I did. We had our season finale against Delaware State coming up, and I wanted to end my college career on a high note before I started looking toward the NFL Draft.

Little did I know at the time that a visit from an NFL scout that week would not only leave me questioning my speed, my size, my tackling ability—everything—it would also set me on a course to fully embracing my third rule to overcoming the odds.

A few days after the awful Bethune-Cookman game, my phone buzzed in the morning. It was Howard's offensive coordinator, A.C. Cauthorn, and by that time, I was used to Coach calling me in the middle of the week; he'd often tell me when an NFL scout was at Howard to watch practice, and he'd tell me to come down and introduce myself before my classes.

I generally looked forward to these visits with scouts. It was a reminder that my dream of playing in the NFL was closer than ever, and it always provided me with confidence and motivation. This visit would be no different—or at least I thought it wouldn't. When I walked into the office to meet the scout from the Atlanta Falcons that was here to see me that way, I had no way of knowing that this guy was gonna rip me the way he did.

I greeted the scout, and he asked to watch some film with me. When I saw him reach for the Bethune-Cookman tape, I thought to myself, "Damn, all those great games I played, and he just had to pick the worst tape of my career. Oh well. I figured he'd know it was an aberration, right?

Wrong. Because as soon as the tape started rolling—and I mean as soon as it started rolling—this guy started talking to me like I'd never played a down of football in my life.

"You miss too many tackles."

"You have bad tackling form."

"You take bad angles."

Not a great start to the meeting. I hoped he'd put in another tape. Maybe that stuff was true in that game, but it wasn't indicative of who I was as a player—I was about to be a three-time Black College All-American. But none of that mattered at this very moment.

"What you think you gonna run in the 40?" he asked.

Look, I'm an honest dude. I could have easily said 4.3. But I said high 4.4s, low 4.5s, to be safe, since the electronic testing the NFL uses to gauge player speed is notoriously slower than hand-timed marks.

His face frowned up.

"Seriously? You look like you run a low 4.6, 4.7. You look slow."

Then, before I could even process that information, he hit me with a roundhouse to the gut.

"What you're showing on film right now, you not gonna make it in the league."

That last one hit me like a ton of bricks. Damn! It's only one game, I thought to myself.

This continued for about 15 minutes, and I'm telling you, this dude was killing me. It was so bad that my defensive backs coach, Ron Bolton, even rose out of his seat in his nearby office and stood in the doorway to listen. I'll never forget the look he had on his face. It was a real confused look, like he wanted to say, "Really?"

When this interview finally came to an end, I was hot. The scout got up and left, and I shook his hand. After that, I spent a few moments alone with Coach Bolton, who I could always count on to give me the truth. Did this scout's assessment mean my NFL goal had been a pipe dream all along?

"Nah, man, don't worry about that," Coach Bolton said. "That guy doesn't know what he's talking about. He ain't have to do all that."

That made me feel better, but as I got up and left, I felt the anger rising in my soul again. That scout really had me feeling like I wasn't ever gonna play in the league. I had a few classes to attend before practice that day, but I was so angry I said "eff" class and went back to my room, laid down, and watched TV.

Right then and there, I started thinking. If the scout was thinking that way about me because of one game, was everyone else in the NFL doing the same? It was a moment for me to sit back and reflect on what was gonna happen next in my life, and whether everything I'd done to get to that point was even worth it.

As I stared at the television, I thought about how I'd gone from being an underrecruited and unranked 170-pound linebacker as a high school senior to earning a full ride and becoming a starting safety at a D-1AA school as a true sophomore, and how I'd done it by running and lifting and studying the game relentlessly, even during the times I didn't want to, all in the name of a dream nobody originally believed was possible for me.

Was all that for nothing? I asked myself. I slunk into my bed and took a deep breath. To find the answer, I'd only have to dive into my past to remember how I'd earned the starting safety job at Howard in the first place.

Entering the 2003 season, we already had a couple starters at safety in Brian Johnson, a junior, and Vontrae Long a senior. Both were pretty good players—Vontrae was even the Mid-Eastern Athletic Conference Freshman of the Year in 2000. I did all I could during training camp to win a starting job, but I couldn't beat either of them out.

It was disappointing, but I made sure to stay ready. The first game of the year comes, we're playing Texas Southern. At the end of the second quarter, B-Johnson—one of my good friends—pulls his hammy. Coach Bolton turns to me and says, "Bethea, you're in." I was a little nervous, and things were moving fast so early on, but once I got that first tackle, the game just slowed down and I was just out there flying around. I finished the game with 10 tackles, and that was only in the second half. I felt great. My dad was listening to the game on the radio, and after the game, he was like, "Boy, you had a hell of a game." He was really excited for me, and so was my mom.

After the way I played in that game, I knew I could play at Howard. I knew I belonged there. And the timing couldn't have been better, because the next week we were playing our rivals, Hampton—the fake HU—in the "Battle of the Real HU." And yes, I had an obvious chip on my shoulder. This school was right down the street from my hometown—literally 15 minutes away—and they never tried to recruit me.

It was my first full start, and it turned out to be one of the best games I played at Howard University. I was amped up, man. My family and friends came up to D.C. to watch the game. We lost 17-14, but that game was in slow motion for me the whole time. I was seeing everything, and I felt as though I was making all the plays. I want to say I had 12 tackles, three fumble recoveries, and one touchdown. That was the game I established myself as a force to be reckoned with in the MEAC, and Coach Bolton was right there to let me know it.

"You had a hell of a game, boy," he told me. "That's the way you play ball."

Around that time is when my coaches and teammates started calling me "Deuce." When I was growing up in high school, everybody used to call me 'Toine and up until that point at Howard, people called me by my last name, Bethea. But "Deuce" was a dope nickname, and it was fitting because I started wearing No. 2 that year after rocking No. 25 as a freshman.

It just so happens that Deion Sanders, one of my biggest football influences growing up, wore No. 2 at Florida State. I liked watching him, along with guys like Ronnie Lott and Rod Woodson, and on the field, I'd like to think Deuce has a little bit of all of those guys. Deuce is a go-hard, no-bullshit type of player, and regardless of my stature—remember, I was 175 pounds as a freshman and 185 as a sophomore—I wanted to make sure my presence is felt on the field and always go balls out, period.

B-Johnson would eventually heal up, but my aggressive on-field attitude and relentless effort helped me remain a starter for the rest of my career at Howard. Every time I stepped on the field, whether it was practice or a game, I made a habit of remembering where I came from, and how the odds had always been against me. It was easy for "Deuce" to come out when I remembered that none of the big schools wanted me, and I didn't even get a full scholarship out of high school. And the way

I saw it, every time I finished a game with a bunch of tackles, I was sticking it to everyone who didn't believe in me coming out of high school.

And as my career at Howard matured and I started to get more accolades, the belief that maybe, just maybe, I could play in the NFL, only grew. To do it, I realized I might never be able to stop using slights as my motivating force.

Proving all my doubters wrong, I realized, felt too satisfying.

While I was very much focused on becoming the best player I could be at Howard, you never want to let your job consume you so much that you never take time to enjoy it. And honestly, one of the best things about playing organized football—just like working with a group of people in any field—is the bond you create with them as you go through the ups and downs of everyday life together. I'll always remember the times I shared with my guys at Howard, and to this day, there are two hilarious stories from back then that we always tell when we get around each other that still make all of us die laughing.

The first happened in 2004, my junior year. We had an assistant coach named James Moses that went to Howard and played there, and when he played, the team was really good. When I was there, we had a lot of talent, but it wasn't correlating into wins. We were mediocre, going .500 a lot, and this coach was sick of it.

So, he was talking to us one time after a loss that year—we ended up finishing 6-5 that season (our best record of my four-year tenure there, by the way)—and he was really pissed off. And when he got mad, his small, round eyes often protruded from his eye sockets, almost like a frog.

Maybe you can see where I'm going with this.

Anyway, we were in a team meeting when he walked up to the front of the room and started cursing us out in an attempt to motivate us and finally get us to start playing to our potential, a common scene in many college locker rooms, I'm sure.

"Y'all some sorry motherfuckers!" he began, his frog eyes beginning to widen and fill with rage. "Y'all walking around here with these Howard football t-shirts on, trying to get all these bitches. Y'all soft as fuck!"

"All y'all Clark Kent motherfuckers, y'all walk around with these shirts on, then go in the phone booth and put these pads on and y'all ain't shit!"

He's cursing us out, and his eyes are growing wider, and it's kinda funny to us, even though we're like damn, he's got a point—we've got a lotta talent but we ain't really doing what we're supposed to be doing on the field.

So finally, after a few minutes, Coach Moses got done cursing us out and he started walking out the door. And I'll never forget this: he might have taken one or two steps out the door when one of my teammates, a real quiet, mild-mannered guy—Mike Brown—says out loud what we're all thinking:

"Ribbit!"

You know, the sound a frog makes.

Man, you should have seen the way Coach Moses opened that door and stormed back into the room.

"Which one of you motherfuckers said it?!" he said, his eyes widening more than ever as we tried to stifle our laughter. "I'll beat your motherfucking ass if you say it again!"

Nobody said anything else, of course. But man, talk about a funny moment. When we got out of the coach's earshot, we all died laughing.

Another funny moment like that came a year later, during my senior season, when we went down to Savannah State for a road game. Now remember, Howard isn't some big D-1 school like Ohio State or Virginia Tech. So we always took bus trips, which wasn't great, but we learned how to make the most of those long bus rides, mainly by sneaking liquor and beer on the trip. We'd pack them up in our bags, and on this particular trip, I'd remember that every time we hit a bump, we'd hear the bottles in the bag clinking. This goes on for hours and hours, but Coach

Petty never said anything, so we get there and we're thinking we're cool or whatever.

We play Savannah State and we win the game 39-21. It was a great team win—one of only four we had that year—so you know we were gonna celebrate. On the way back, we were on the bus, sipping it up. With the coaches on the other bus, we figured we were safe to party a little bit. We did it discreetly and were careful not to pour the drinks in plain view, so we thought we were being slick.

Anyway, the bus stopped for a bathroom break, when Coach comes onto our bus and demands us to give him our attention. He had a real stern look on his face like he always did—his straight face was legendary, you could never really tell when he was joking or serious—and he began to address us.

"Good team win, fellas," he yelled. "But, yeah, I heard y'all mother-fuckers got drinks on this bus!"

We we're all like shit, we're busted. And then he smiled.

"The next time y'all motherfuckers have drinks on this bus and don't offer me none, I'mma run all y'all motherfuckers!"

Man, as soon as he said that, we pulled every bottle we had out, like here you go, Coach! And to this day, me and the guys, we laugh at that. And whenever we go back to D.C. and link up with coach, we'll joke on him about that, too. Man, those were good times.

But back in my room, only hours after that scout shitted on me, I wasn't thinking about the good times, funny stories, or anything like that—I was still hot about what the scout had said.

As practice time quickly approached, I realized that I had to make a decision. I could either keep feeling sorry for myself and pack it in, or, I could pull myself out of the funk, drag my ass to practice, and prove that guy wrong. There were no other options, And for me, there really was no choice.

After all, hadn't people been doubting me as a football player my whole life? Have I ever once let their opinion of me affect my effort in pursuit of my dream? Hell, no. So why would I start now? Screw that guy. I was going to do what I'd always done—take his slight and use it as fuel for my personal fire so I could rise to the occasion when the opportunity presented itself.

I hopped out of bed, headed over to Greene Stadium and practiced my ass off that day. It was no different, really, than the way I pushed myself through workouts my freshman year at Howard, despite the fact that I went unrecruited my senior year at Denbigh and didn't even have a full ride at the time.

After practice, I knew I was on the right track when Coach Bolton gave me some quiet words of confidence—on the field, no less.

"Deuce, just keep doing what you're doing," he told me. "You're gonna be fine."

A few days later, I went out and had a hell of a game in my final college contest, snatching two interceptions in a 23-7 loss to Delaware State. That scout's critique of me fueled my performance that day, and I sure hoped he saw it.

In retrospect, I guess I can say I appreciate how direct the scout was. Sure, he was wrong about me, but in a way, he did help me harness one of the core philosophies I'd use to prove people wrong in my career, over and over again.

But life is funny, as I'm sure you know. As it turns out, I'd get to see that scout again only three months later, and the timing of that chance meeting—which came before the biggest test of my professional life, the 2006 NFL Combine—really couldn't have been better.

After my final college game, I quickly picked an agent. I was going to go all-in on my NFL dream, and I chose Adisa Bakari to be my guy. What struck me and my parents was how real and honest he was; he didn't promise I'd be a first or second-round pick. In fact, he said I might be a sixth or seventh-round pick or undrafted free agent. But he liked the way I played ball, and that's why he came to see me. At the time, he didn't have many big-name players, but we clicked and I liked what he was saying.

Soon after that, I decided to go to Atlanta to start training for the NFL Combine, the biggest, most time-consuming job interview in professional football. There, along with 300 other players, I'd be subjected to a number of interviews with teams, not to mention a thorough medical checkup and a ton of position drills and physical tests, like the bench press and 40-yard dash.

Like most defensive backs in attendance, the latter was what I was most concerned about. Every young defensive back who wants to make it to the league knows that the 40-yard dash can either make or break you. Guys get drafted higher or lower than they should every year just because of their 40, and if you're a small-school underdog like me, the stakes were much higher. A slow 40 would give scouts and teams all the reason they need to write you off as a guy the big schools were right to pass on.

So, honestly, I trained my ass off. At the end of my senior year at Howard, I weighed 187 pounds, but by the time the Combine came around three months later, I weighed 203 pounds—the heaviest I've ever been. That was a nice weight for someone who could play either safety or corner, which some teams were looking at me to play, and I was also running in the high 4.4s and low 4.5s during training—solid enough to get drafted, I thought, but not spectacular.

All this swarmed my mind in late February of 2006, when I walked to the starting line on the field at the RCA Dome to run the first of two 40s. While you're there, all you could see is the hard, green turf in front of you and the hundreds of NFL scouts and executives in the stands, evaluating your every move.

It's nerve-wracking for some, but as I stood at the starting line, gathering my breaths for the biggest run of my life, I scanned the stands for the first time and I saw him—the scout that crushed me three months earlier, sitting there in the front row, watching.

Wild story, I know. All those people in attendance, and *that's* the guy I see at that exact moment?

Come on.

If I hadn't been so well-versed in using slights as motivation, maybe the sight of that guy would have unnerved me. But you know me by now. Now that I saw him, I was getting pissed all over again. All those old feelings of anger rushed back, and as I crouched into my stance, ready to explode 40 yards downfield, I remembered everything that dude said about me—how I was too slow, how I couldn't tackle, how I'd never make it. So I hear the horn, I take off, and I was moving, man. I was flying. When it was over, I couldn't wait to find out what I'd run.

I had my cell phone in a nearby bag, and after I finished, I ran over to it and texted one of my homeboys—Howard defensive tackle Jesse Hayes, a.k.a. "Big Cheese"—who was watching from home, to find out what I'd run.

He texted back quickly: 4.39.

Wow. To this day, that time still amazes me. Talk about rising to the occasion, man! That was a great time, on the high end of anything I'd ever run before with an electronic time. Understand, most players run in the 4.4s and 4.5s. Some players who play my position even run in the 4.6s and 4.7s.

But in the 4.3s? That's cornerback speed, and I knew it would raise my draft stock, especially for the teams that were interested in me as a cornerback. I knew I had to run it again, to prove it wasn't a fluke, and minutes later I ended up posting a 4.41—another strong time.

That was easily the high point of the Combine for me, which makes for a long, long weekend. You're getting up early in the morning, you're getting poked and prodded by doctors, you're being interviewed by all those teams. I'm excited to be able to say I experienced it, though. I think that Combine kind of helped me out a little bit, put me on the map. I was in the top five at my position in the 40 and bench press, and my vertical and broad jumps were great. That was my first time measuring myself against the so-called big dogs and D-1 guys, and I saw I was right there with them.

By the time my pro day at Howard rolled around, I started hearing I could go as high as the third round, and that was definitely exciting. The spring before my senior year, Ron Bartell—who started next to me in Howard's secondary in 2004—got drafted in the second round to the Rams. So did Nick Collins, another HBCU safety who went to Bethune-Cookman and got drafted by the Packers. So I'm like, if it happened for them, it can happen for me, too.

I should have known that my path to the NFL wasn't gonna be that easy, however. For the underdog, it never is.

Back then, the NFL Draft was a two-day event—not the three-day affair it is now. The first, second, and third rounds were on a Saturday, and the last four rounds were held the next day.

Because I had been getting some third-round buzz, I decided to watch the whole thing, starting with the first round on Saturday. If my name was getting called that day, you can be damn sure I was gonna see it. I gathered with a bunch of my friends and family at my parents' house in Newport News to watch it.

Once the draft started, my hopes to be selected early rose as I saw safeties—Michael Huff, Donte Whitner, and Jason Allen—going off the board left and right. Then we get into the second round, and Daniel Bullocks, Daniel Manning, and Roman Harper got taken, too.

Now we get to the end of the second round, and the Minnesota Vikings are up at pick No. 64. The tight ends coach for the Vikings at the time was Jimmie Johnson, a Howard alum, and he'd already told one of my college coaches that they were thinking of either picking me or quarterback Tarvaris Jackson from Alabama State, also a HBCU.

But shortly before their pick came up, he called one of my college coaches—James Moses—who then relayed to me what Coach Johnson said, and how upset he was.

"Man, I was just talking to Jimmie and he was saying Minnesota was talking about taking you, but a trespassing charge popped up on your record," Coach Moses told me.

And man, I'm not gonna lie—I was in shock. I'd also had a DUI in college—and we'll get to that later in the book, I promise—but I was upfront about that with teams I'd met with, and everyone knew about it. The trespassing charge, though? That was really, really petty, and that shit—which happened during Thanksgiving break of my junior year while I was in Newport News—was supposed to be expunged off my record. That's why I didn't bring it up to scouts or my coaches.

But as we all know, NFL teams can find anything and everything they want about you, and they went and found it. And as I started to wonder if some B.S. like that would keep me from being drafted, Adisa went into overdrive explaining to teams what happened.

The incident occurred in November of 2004. It was Thanksgiving break, and you know around that time, everybody's coming home from college. So me and my boys headed to this club called Mitty's, which is now closed. But back in the day, it was one of the clubs that was poppin' at the time in Newport News.

Now at the time, Mitty's had a real strict dress code. No baggy shirts, no baggy jeans—real crazy. My homeboy who drove couldn't get in because of the dress code, so he's like, "Cool, I'll go to the crib, and I'll come back up here to grab y'all when you let out". So we go in and have a good time—a great time, actually—when a big fight, a big melee, breaks out. People are in there fighting, breaking bottles, throwing chairs. Someone I knew there even got stabbed in the neck. Crazy, right?

Me and my homeboys, Nell and Gentry, go outside with everybody, and police are trying to get everything situated, everything calmed down. But instead of us hopping in a ride with somebody else we knew that was there, we called our homeboy and said, "Look, come get us. It's crazy out here." And he's like, "I'm on my way."

So we're still in the parking lot, waiting on our ride, and the police had already told us one time to get out the parking lot. We started to walk out of the parking lot toward the gas station across the street while we waited for the one guy to pick us up, but the cop said we weren't moving fast enough, and he ran up on us again.

"Didn't I tell y'all to leave the parking lot?" he said.

We tried to explain to him that our ride wasn't there yet, but he wasn't trying to hear that. So now he's got me and my two homeboys on the car—they threw us in cuffs—and it's another melee, and the cops are agitated. Now my homeboy who drove is finally pulling up and we're trying to explain to the cops that he's here now, but the cop wasn't trying to hear that.

"Get in the car!" he yelled.

So when I said earlier this trespassing charge was petty, I meant it. We ended up in jail for a few hours that night, even though we didn't do much. When I got to the jail with my two homeboys, Nell tried to call his sister to get us out, but she didn't answer. And then Gentry said there was no way his mom was coming.

So my mom was the last resort if we wanted to get out of there, which didn't make it any easier. I did not want to make that call, even though I didn't do anything wrong. I just knew she was going to be mad.

Even still, when she picked up the phone, I was grateful. Anything beats a night in jail, I thought to myself before I proceeded to tell her where I was.

"I'm downtown," I said.

"Okay," she said, matter-of-factly.

"Naw, mom, I'm locked up. I need y'all to come get me."

And she's like, "What?"

Remember, me and my brother like to play tricks on my mom by making her think we'd gotten in trouble when we really didn't. (No, we didn't stop doing it, even after his incident at Delaware State.) So she didn't believe me when I told her at first.

"No, Mom, I'm serious," I pleaded.

My dad was a deputy sheriff in Newport News at the time and worked at the jail. Eventually, they came and got us after a couple of hours in the joint. Amazingly, after I told my parents what happened, neither one of them were mad because they realized it was a B.S. charge.

I was initially charged with trespassing, but the charge was thrown out and I never had to go to court or anything for it. We were also told that it would not go on my record, and that's why we thought there was nothing for me to tell the scouts about regarding the trespassing charge.

So, look, I don't know what type of research the Vikings did, but for them to dig that up, it's crazy. That's why, to this day, I tell the kids that you've got to keep your nose clean, because if people want to dig up stuff on you, they will find it.

With some newfound questions about my background muddying up the draft waters, the Vikings ended up picking Tarvaris to close out the second round, and the draft proceeded to the third round, which closed with the Jets taking safety Eric Smith—the ninth safety of the day to be taken.

At that point, I'm not gonna lie—I was hurting, wondering, damn, did I mess up my opportunity? My friends and family told me not to worry about, but as the second day of the draft commenced, and the fourth and fifth rounds went without me being taken, nothing was really shaking, though a couple of teams had started calling my agent, telling him they were interested in bringing me in as a high-priority free agent signee if I didn't get drafted. Damn.

And then, finally, I get the call from Bill Polian, the Hall of Fame general manager of the Indianapolis Colts, who had the second-to-last pick in the sixth round.

"Hello, Antoine. This is Bill Polian," he began. "We're about to draft you with the 207th pick. Would you love to be a Colt?"

"Yes, sir," I told him.

"Alright, I'm gonna put you on the phone with Coach Dungy."

At the time, I stepped outside to talk to future Hall of Famer Tony Dungy, and right at that time, my name flashed across the bottom of the screen and everybody at the house went crazy. They came running outside, they came hugging me, and I'm on the phone, talking to Coach Dungy about when rookie minicamp would be and when they were gonna fly me out.

I had some boys there I grew up with and we were all in the front yard going crazy. They eventually ran to the mall and bought all the Colts hats they could find and came back to the house. We rented out a room in one of our local bars and invited some people to come out. It was a good time. The celebration was worth the wait.

Well, almost. The truth is, I was taken on day two of the draft, in round six, with pick 207, and those are some numbers I'll never forget, just a few more reasons to have a chip on my shoulder.

So understand, when I encourage people to take every slight personally, I mean it. And no, I don't mean it in a sense where you're walking around making excuses, putting the blame on others and feeling sorry for yourself. When I say take slights personally, I mean that you use those doubts to fuel your work.

And I mean that literally, too. Have you ever felt overlooked? Undervalued? Remember it when you're working and use it work harder.

Have you ever been denied, abandoned or rejected? That's when you take it personal and fight back with action by remembering it when you're working to help you work harder. Remember, the only limitations that exist are those in which you impose on yourself. And trust me, the greatest pleasure in life is doing what people say you cannot do! Know this: you can only control what you can control, so take it personal, then take control and retaliate by putting it into your work.

Thirteen seasons later, I've outlasted every one of the safeties that were taken ahead of me in the draft, and a big reason why I was able to do that is because I fully embraced the importance of using these types of slights as motivation—in the exact way I've outlined it.

Want proof? Well, you might think it's funny, but honestly, I can remember the names of most—if not all—the 20 safeties who were taken in front of me. I can't forget those names. No knock on them, but for me, it was a stiff reminder that I was still the underdog and that many people were still counting me out just because I went to a small school and they doubted the level of talent we played against.

So now I had this opportunity to play in the National Football League, and all I kept telling myself was, "Alright 'Toine, what are you gonna do with it?" I had all the motivation I needed to go show and prove what I could do. But making it in the NFL as an underdog is about more than "want-to"—it's about taking advantage of any sliver of opportunity that is put in front of you.

Fortunately, I was going to a championship-caliber organization in Indianapolis where the concept of getting your job done, no matter what, was stressed on a daily basis, which I'd soon learn was no coincidence.

RULE #4

No Excuses, No Explanations

My INSIDES CHURNED AS I stood upright on the sideline, periodically peering upward as I tried to comprehend the mere size of the cavernous, sold-out stadium.

This was September 10, 2006—the very first regular season game of my NFL career—and at that point, I had long grown accustomed to having that uncomfortable feeling in the moments right before a football game. Considering the inherent violence that was sure to take place over the next three hours—and given the way I loved to hit, the role I'd likely play in it—only a fool wouldn't feel some butterflies beforehand.

It was a balmy, clear fall night in Secaucus, New Jersey. Based on the way those butterflies continued to flutter in my stomach as I proceeded to make mistake after mistake throughout the first half, I began to feel something completely foreign to me, a feeling I hadn't felt since ... hell, way back when I was kid, when my mother and brother stared down death and won ...

Nervousness, mixed with a little bit of fear.

It was understandable, I guess. At the time, this was the biggest game of my life. As if starting my professional career on Sunday Night Football against the New York Giants—the premier team in one of the league's biggest markets—facing the biggest crowd (78,000-plus) I'd ever played in front of wasn't nerve-wracking enough, the media had spent weeks hyping this game as the "Manning Bowl," since our quarterback, Peyton Manning, and the Giants' quarterback, Eli Manning, were brothers.

To me, that meant that everyone in the NFL would be watching this game, and by proxy, that meant everyone would be watching me—Antoine Bethea, a sixth-round pick from a small-school HBCU—make his first career NFL start at free safety.

As confident as I was (and am) in my own ability, I admit there was a part of me that couldn't believe I was out there, playing on national television at the age of 22. I'm the same guy that didn't even have a Rivals profile, the same guy that had zero Division 1 offers coming from high school. Now here I was, on the field with the likes of bona fide stars like Peyton Manning, Marvin Harrison, Dwight Freeney, and Robert Mathis.

To me, the fact that it only took me four months to earn the starting job after the Colts drafted me was validation for all the work I put in, a sweet victory over all the people who—by ignoring me for so long—were essentially telling me what they thought I couldn't do. NFL scouts. College recruiters. Front offices. I had a burning desire to show them all.

Even still, I was far from satisfied. You know that old saying of the NFL standing for "not for long?" It's true. And that night against the Giants—after I spent the first half forgetting easy stuff, stuff I had been doing since I was at Howard, stuff I had been doing through OTAs—I knew that if I didn't want to get benched, I'd better get it together, and quick.

Fortunately, we led 16-7 at halftime, which meant my leash was a little longer than it might have otherwise been. I was also fortunate that by then, I'd fully bought into a can't-miss team motto that proved to be so crucial on my journey toward winning the starting job—and ultimately, my veteran teammates' respect—that it would eventually become my fourth rule to overcoming the odds.

Shortly after I arrived in Indianapolis following the NFL Draft, I knew I was in for a real battle just to make the roster. The Colts had seven safeties on the roster at the time—myself, Bob Sanders, Mike Doss, Mike Giordano, Dexter Reid, Gerome Sapp, and fellow rookie Antwan Marsh—and when we started practicing together for the first during organized team activities in May, I was number six on the depth chart. No lie.

So yeah, I recognized quickly I definitely had my work cut out for me. But honestly, I was just thrilled to slip on that brand-new Colts helmet every day. It was really a dream come true, man, and what's more, I'm making more money than I ever thought I'd see. My signing bonus was $50,000, my base salary was $225,000, and shit, I was good with it, especially given where I came from.

All that made it easy to approach my new opportunity with lots of enthusiasm. And what's cool was, when I arrived for rookie minicamp, I quickly realized I already had a familiarity with the Cover 2-heavy defense they were running, since it was the same thing we ran at Howard. My new defensive backs coach in Indy was teaching me the same techniques Coach Bolton had already taught me at Howard, so I was able to step in and make plays quickly.

After making some plays in the rookie minicamp, the coaches started rotating me in with the first string when the vets arrived in May, and I'm proud to say I even picked off Peyton a couple times. Doing that was an "I belong" moment; he was in his prime at that time, and by being able to get my hands on the ball, I knew I was doing something right. My confidence continued to grow—I just needed to keep moving in that direction.

"You're good in helmets and shorts," Alan Williams, my defensive backs coach, told me before we broke for a month in late June. "But can you come out here and do the same thing in training camp, when there's tackling? If so, you have a good chance to make this team."

Now to myself, I'm thinking: That's what I do best—tackle. And once we get to training camp in July, I proved it. Michael Doss, the starter at free safety, got banged up, and I kept getting more time with the first-string in his place. Things are going well, and I'm getting the sense I won't just make the team—I'll actually start.

Then, in practice one day, we're in the red zone when Peyton throws a spiral up the seam to tight end Dallas Clark. I jump in the air to try to knock it down, but he runs under me and hits my leg. I fall to the ground—my knee is feeling funny—and when I get back to the sideline, trying to cut on it, my knee gives out on me. I'm terrified that I tore some cartilage in my knee, which would have knocked me out for the whole season.

Fortunately, it was just a sprained MCL, and I was back in two weeks, just in time for the second preseason game against the Seattle Seahawks. I played a good, solid half against them, and I do the next week against New Orleans, when I recovered a fumble on a kickoff and intercepted a pass.

"Yo, you good, young boy, you good—you ballin'," I remember one of my old heads telling me.

I knew better than to take it for granted, though, even after they took me out after a series in the fourth and final preseason game—treatment reserved solely for starters. Doss was back by that point, and with All-Pro Bob Sanders locking down the other safety spot, I had no idea how much I'd play, even though I figured I'd made the team at that point.

Imagine my elation when, the week before the regular season opener against the Giants, my defensive backs coach called me into his office and told me I'm going to be the starting free safety in Week 1. Man, talk about happy. It was sweeter than the day I was drafted, and just as sweet—if not sweeter—than the day Coach Petty called me into his office three years earlier and told me I'd finally earned my full ride at Howard.

Going into that year, all I'd wanted to do was make the team. Now here I was, getting ready to start the "Manning Bowl" on national television. Even I couldn't have imagined that four years prior.

In retrospect, I realize I couldn't have done it without some good fortune. And the biggest break I got was being drafted by an organization that knew how to nurture young players.

That is not a given at this level, by the way. These are grown men with families, and when a team brings in a younger, cheaper player—like myself at the time—it isn't uncommon for vets to see these guys as competition, someone who is there to take food off their kids' table, not as teammates.

This wasn't a problem for the Colts, however. Although rookies had to earn the vets' respect in other ways—we'll get to that later—Coach Dungy made sure the veterans didn't overtly haze the young guys. While guys on other teams had to sing in front of the team (and worse), the worst we had to do was grab some food for the vets or carry some pads. That's it.

"Hey, these young guys are going to help us win," Coach Dungy used to say. "We need to make them feel welcome."

For the most part, they did, even though you still had some vets that didn't want to talk to the young guys. I get it—guys are protective of their turf—but I will say this: most of my older teammates on the Colts were cool as hell, largely because Coach Dungy truly preached a family atmosphere.

While every NFL coach talks about "family, family, family," few truly walked the walk like Coach Dungy. Other coaches talk it, but they'll have you in the training facility all day, keeping you away from your family. But Coach preached balance, and I noticed that our coaches not only brought their wives and kids around all the time, they weren't working crazy 17-hour days or whatever.

This attitude trickled down to the players, many of whom took Coach's words to heart. Take our star quarterback, Peyton Manning, for instance. When I first arrived in Indianapolis, I didn't have a car yet, so one day, only weeks after I became a Colt, I remember standing outside of the practice facility, waiting for the shuttle to come pick me up so I could go back to the hotel I was staying at.

That's when Peyton, who was a 30-year-old five-time All-Pro by then, walked by me, saw me standing there and asked me if I needed a ride to the hotel.

"Yeah," I said.

It's a little thing, I know, but there are a lot of established guys who wouldn't do something like that. During that short drive to the hotel, I took advantage of the time I spent with him, picking his brain about what I could expect in the league and the kind of "tells" he looks for from safeties when trying to diagnose the defense pre-play. He actually gave me a really detailed answer, which shouldn't be a surprise, given how cerebral he was.

It's things like that made Peyton a very good leader. He was detail-oriented, obsessed with perfection, and no one worked harder or studied the game more. Guys had to follow his lead.

But he was far from the only veteran who embraced me. On defense, a trio of starters—defensive end Robert Mathis, inside linebacker Gary Brackett, and outside linebacker Cato June—were great to me. It should come as no surprise that I had a ton in common with all those guys, starting with being an underdog.

Rob, for one, was an undersized, late-round pick from a historical black college, just like me—the Colts took him as a 6-foot-2, 245-pound defensive end in the fifth round from Alabama A&M in 2003—so he knew how hard it was to get to the NFL from where we came. That dude welcomed me to the mix from the get-go, often shouting "black college, baby!" when I made a play in practice or college my rookie year.

Meanwhile, Cato went to a big state school—the University of Michigan—but he was also a late-round pick (the Colts took him in the sixth round in 2003) from D.C., so he knew all about Howard. GB, meanwhile, also went to a big state school (Rutgers), but he didn't even get drafted when he came out in 2003.

Early in my rookie year, all those guys were quick to offer me any advice they could to help me shine. When I first got there, I kept to myself, scoping out the scene—when I go somewhere new, I like to see how people act and then react accordingly—but I grew pretty comfortable as soon as I realized that if you work hard and make plays, the vets will accept you.

The team's motto—no excuses, no explanations—was plastered everywhere in the practice facility, including on a wall in the locker room. And after passing it every day, you had no choice but to see it. Guys really bought into it, too, and the message was everything to me that year. It simply meant that on this team, regardless of the circumstances, if you're on the field, you're expected to get your job done, period. And if you don't, you shut up, figure it out and get it right the next time.

I thought about that team motto as I sat in the locker room during halftime of our season opener, and I resolved to get myself squared away. The vets, supportive as always, slapped my shoulder pads as they encouraged me on the way out of the tunnel.

"Man, you gon' be good," one told me. "Just do what you do."

I bounced back well in the second half, cutting down the mental blocks and finishing the game strong with six tackles. We won the game 26-21, and my one of my coaches was impressed that I'd self-corrected my issues.

"No excuses, no explanations," I thought to myself.

"Ain't no telling where I may be/May see me in D.C. at Howard Homecoming"
Notorious B.I.G., *Kick In The Door*

Although the Colts' team motto was pretty unforgiving—do your job, no matter what—that didn't mean we didn't have a good time now and then. On the contrary, actually. You know the saying, "Work hard, play hard"? Well, that fit us.

And honestly, I think that's important. Playing in the NFL is fun, but as the season went on, I learned that it comes with a lot of pressure. We needed to let off steam sometimes, and believe me, we did.

As a young guy, a 22-year-old rookie, I'm not going to lie, I had a blast enjoying the nightlife back then. I never trusted people easily— that's the Newport News in me—but I did enjoy going to parties and being around people, if that makes sense. In fact, I think that's one of the reasons I got along so well with so many of the veterans when I was just a rookie.

Well, that and the fact that I introduced many of them to Howard's homecoming that October. For real. See, Howard's homecoming is so much fun, it has taken on an almost-mythical status among many in the African-American community. Held every October, Howard alumni and celebrities alike regularly return to Washington, D.C., to enjoy the large variety of parties and star-studded concerts that make the whole thing pop. Rappers like Drake, Jay Z, Tupac, and Biggie—among others—have all performed there, and it's just a great time.

Luckily for me, our bye week as a rookie—October 15—was located right in the middle of Howard's homecoming. I couldn't wait to see some of my old teammates, so there was no way I was missing that. Cato knew how dope homecoming was—remember, he went to high school in D.C.—and he decided to go, too. And since Cato and Reggie Wayne were tight, Reggie came along with my friends, second-year cornerbacks Marlin Jackson and Kelvin Hayden.

We all had a little money at the time, obviously, so we decided to do it big. We stayed at a nice hotel, and while you might think I was nervous about essentially hosting all these vets for their bye week vacations—which NFL players treasure more than you could imagine—I wasn't concerned at all because I knew it would be dope.

We all got there on a Thursday, and I threw a little party that night at a local club. The next day, I took them to Yardfest, an outdoor concert held on "The Yard" that still goes on to this day. Many legendary rappers have performed on that stage, and I still chuckle at the way my Colts teammates—all of whom went to big state schools—looked when they saw all the beautiful black women out there.

"Damn, 'Toine!" one of them said.

We had a blast the next few nights, as I took them to some parties at some popular D.C. nightspots. And on Sunday, while the other vets flew back to Indianapolis—we had to be at the facility by 1 p.m. Monday to lift weights—me and Cato were having so much fun we decided to stay an extra night and just catch an early flight to Indianapolis this next morning. We got there in time for weightlifting, too.

That's a pretty good example of how we had our fun, but always managed to still take care of our responsibilities. "No excuses, no explanations" wasn't just a team motto, it was a way of life.

We were human, after all. And while I can honestly say our tendency to enjoy the nightlife very rarely impacted us on the field, there's one instance where we all know that it did.

By the middle of November, I was still the starting free safety, and we were rolling on our march to the Super Bowl. We opened the season 9-0, and we even started to think we had a chance to go undefeated.

Then came a November 19 road test against Dallas ... which, unfortunately for us, coincided with Reggie's and Cato's birthdays. Reggie was turning 28 that Saturday and Cato was turning 27 that Friday. Given how well we were doing as a team, they definitely wanted to take advantage, since winning seasons always make for awesome parties (everyone loves to be associated with a winner, it turns out).

That Friday—two days before the Dallas game—they decided to hold a party at Indiana Pacers center Jermaine O'Neal's club in downtown Indy. They were promoting it all week long, and you know it was a big deal because it got back to Coach Dungy.

"Yeah, I heard about this big party," Coach Dungy told us that week. "I know everybody's going to be there, so make sure you drive safe or make sure you get a driver. I don't want *anybody* late to Saturday meetings."

Coach repeated this message over and over again all week, so by the time Friday rolled around, we knew what the situation was. I was just a rookie, but I knew this was party was a big deal when I walked into Club 7 and saw Peyton—who you never really saw in a club—in there, along with other people you wouldn't expect, like Marvin and members of the player personnel staff.

We all felt like rock stars, the entire city came out to party that night. And I'm thinking damn, this is the life! We might have been in Indianapolis, but you couldn't tell me I wasn't in D.C. or New York that night.

Anyway, we end up having a ball. And guess what? The next day, not one person was late … even though it doesn't mean some of us weren't hung over. We all enjoyed making fun of one defensive starter who fell asleep in the defensive meeting, while Coach Dungy—who sat right next to him—just shook his head.

We got on the plane later that day, and it was, by far, the quietest plane ride we ever had. Everybody on that shit was knocked out cold, fast asleep, trying to get their rest. We end up playing a good game in Dallas, but we lose 21-14. And after that, the joke amongst the team was the Dallas Cowboys didn't beat us—it was Reggie Wayne and Cato June's party that did. To this day, man, we laugh at that shit.

Fortunately for us, one loss wasn't about to derail our Super Bowl quest.

Let me tell you something: by the end of the 2006 regular season, I was *tired*. I'd started 14 of 16 regular season games—I missed two due to injury—and four preseason games, giving me a grand total of 18. That was nearly two seasons' worth on the college level. And now, we were going to the playoffs, when the games *really* matter.

But even though my body was killing me, I had more than enough motivation to keep building on a really strong rookie season. I'd finished the regular season with 90 tackles, four passes defended and a pick, but strangely, I still felt like I had more to prove.

A big reason for that was our run defense, which everybody was killing at the time. That wasn't without merit, either; that year, we yielded

173 rushing yards per game, which ranked dead last in the NFL by a good 30 yards per game.

That's why so many people predicted we'd lose our wild card game to the Kansas City Chiefs, even though we finished 12-4 and won our division and were playing at home. The Chiefs had Larry Johnson at running back, a big 230-pound back who'd had a great year, rushing for 1,789 yards and 17 touchdowns, and one of the best offensive lines in football.

But we felt we were being disrespected, and we came out like some dogs, flying around and hitting everything that moved. We ended up stuffing them multiple times on third down while holding L.J. to just 32 yards on 13 carries, and we won the game easily, 23-8. I even got the first playoff interception of my career, which was like icing on the cake.

The next week, we went on the road and won a slugfest with Baltimore, 15-6. Once again, our run defense stood tall, holding the Ravens' rushing offense to only 83 yards all day, and once again I got an interception, the second of my career in the postseason, in front of my family, many of whom made the drive up from Virginia to see me on the big stage.

That set up the game everybody was waiting for—the AFC Championship showdown against our rivals, the New England Patriots. The day before the game, the Chicago Bears won the NFC Championship, and inside we're thinking our game against the Pats is basically the Super Bowl, because there was no way Chicago's quarterback, Rex Grossman, was going to beat us.

So, we come out and ... the Patriots start whipping our tails. I mean, we're at home and they're whipping our asses, 21-6 at halftime.

But the one thing we all appreciated about Coach Dungy was he never, ever panicked. Ever. When he walked in at halftime, he didn't f-bomb anybody, he didn't start cursing. He yelled to get our attention, but only to get us to focus on the details, because we were making too many little mistakes.

I'll give it to the Indy fans, though; they didn't give up on us. It was so loud in the RCA Dome when the Pats were on offense that I could barely hear the defensive call in the huddle—and the man calling the play was only a few feet away. We buckled down, Peyton and the offense got hot, and after we took a 38-34 lead with a minute left, it was up to our defense to hold on.

But New England had Tom Brady, and of course, that was more than a notion. On the fourth play of the drive, we ran Cover 2. Our corners always worked on how, if the quarterback's back is to you, you slide over to cross his face. Marlin did that, Brady threw it his way, and Marlin jumped the route and caught the interception as the crowd exploded.

Let me tell you, that was one of the greatest feelings in the world. Inside, I'm thinking, damn, this time last year I was at Howard University. Now I'm about to go to the Super Bowl in my first year as a pro.

We knew Super Bowl XLI was going to be historic. Thanks to Coach Dungy and the Chicago Bears' coach, Lovie Smith, this marked the first time two black coaches were squaring off in the Super Bowl.

The vets were telling me how lucky I was to be playing in the Super Bowl so early in my career, but I've gotta be honest, I didn't take much heed to what was really happening—I was too busy enjoying the moment. The game was in Miami, the media coverage was crazy, and I was ready to play on football's biggest stage.

Plus, we were pretty confident we were going to win. In our mind, New England was our hurdle. Nothing against the Bears, but we felt like we were better than them.

Even still, after we enjoyed our first two nights in Miami with no curfew on Sunday and Monday, we respected Coach Dungy so much, no one missed curfew as gametime drew near. And our team leaders—led by Peyton, who the media kept talking about never winning the big one—were definitely taking this game seriously.

To that end, I'll never forget the team meeting we held two weeks before the game, when the entire team gathered to nail down the logistics for Super Bowl week. All of us were allowed to bring one person to the meeting—whether it was your wife, significant other, fiancé, girlfriend, whatever—just so nothing could be lost in translation as we all tried to coordinate how the team would help us bring our families down for the game.

Personally, I didn't have anybody with me, as I was single at the time. But lots of guys brought their wives to the meeting, which only added to the craziness of what transpired. When the owner, Jim Irsay, and team president, Bill Polian, got up to speak about the hotel accommodations, it became clear that some of the players wanted their wives to stay with them in the team hotel since it could save them money. But this was a problem for Peyton.

"Man, I don't know how I'm gonna feel having wives and children on the same floor where I'm staying," Peyton said. "I'll be trying to study for the game, and I worry about the noise."

"Okay, that's understandable," Polian replied. "We haven't thought about that, but we'll come back to it."

Well, after about five minutes, he tried to move on to the next topic, and Peyton stood right back up.

"You know what? Let's just make that happen," he said, even more forcefully. "I don't want any kids or wives on the same floor that I'm staying on."

When he sat down, I was like "Oh shit." And inside, I'm like, "Damn, fellas, like, y'all got y'all wives and shit here, y'all gotta say *something*. If they don't stay with you at the hotel, it's gonna cost you guys money!"

And get this—nobody said anything. Not a word. And when we got to our team hotel in Miami, there was not a wife or child in sight on his floor. It was the damnedest thing I'd ever seen, and that's when I knew Peyton had real, legitimate clout in the organization. But heading into the biggest game of our lives, I sure was glad he was on our side.

When I woke up on the day of the Super Bowl—February 4, 2007—I was so excited, I didn't even care about the steady rain that was falling. Even though we were about to play the first-ever Super Bowl in the rain, there was no way we were gonna let that get in the way of our destiny. No excuses, no explanations, remember?

The magnitude of the moment really hit me during the national anthem, as we stood on the sideline while the cascade of lightbulbs flashed from the distance as fans and photographers captured the moment. As a young kid, everybody dreams of going to the Super Bowl and playing in it, so this was one of those "pinch yourself" moments like, damn, I'm here now, and this shit is real.

Coach Dungy, steady as always, had a calming effect on us, as he told us to just play our game.

"Yeah, it's the Super Bowl, but go out there and do what you do," he said. "Whatever we did to get here, that's what we need to do."

Obviously on the defensive side, that meant we had to stop the run. They had a pair of good backs in Cedric Benson and Thomas Jones, but again, Grossman wasn't going to beat us, so we keyed in on taking away their best offensive weapons.

Now, I'm not gonna lie—when Devin Hester opened the game with a kick return touchdown, that definitely stunned us a bit. But from there, it was game on. The offense ran it well, and defensively, we corralled the running game. Once we took a 22-14 lead in the third quarter, we were confident we had it. Again, we had Dwight Freeney and Robert Mathis on the edge, and we didn't believe Grossman could make the throws down the seam against the Cover 2 with those guys rushing him.

We pulled away for good in the fourth quarter, when Kelvin Hayden got a pick-6 on Grossman to give us a 29-17 lead and Bob Sanders intercepted him again to thwart another drive.

When Bob got the pick, we all started to feel giddy, even though 12 minutes remained in the quarter. Grossman was on the ropes, and we were too close to victory to let it slip through our grasp. By the time

9:58 eastern struck, the confetti started raining down on our heads, and we—the Indianapolis Colts—were champions of the world.

I was happy for everybody, especially Peyton and Tony, because people could no longer say they couldn't win the big one. All those years the Colts had spent together, coming up short of this moment, they never made excuses and they never tried to explain it—they just got back to work and got better. I did the same as a rookie, starting with my rocky first start in September, but really, I'd done it my whole life—I just didn't know it.

From the college recruiters that ignored me, to the scout that disrespected me, to the NFL teams that doubted me by letting me fall to the sixth round, I never once made excuses—I just worked harder. It's so simple, yet it's definitely easier said than done.

Just remember, nothing in the world beats persistence. Nothing. When you get tired, keep pushing. There's a reward on the other side!

For me, after the Super Bowl, my reward had arrived. Now, Antoine Bethea, a sixth-round rookie from small-school Howard University with zero Division-1 offers out of high school, was a defensive starter on the Super Bowl champions. As a rookie, no less! Oh yes, it was time to celebrate this journey.

And the best part was, the party was just beginning, as I was about to experience the best three months of my life. But what turned out to be more valuable were the lessons I'd come to realize over the next 13 years, as I still had three more rules I'd come to develop.

Get Good People in your Corner

You sometimes hear players or coaches say they had an empty feeling after winning the Super Bowl, a "what now?" or "is this it?" type of deal. But let me tell you something—the 2006 Indianapolis Colts know nothing about that.

Maybe it was all the close losses in the playoffs in prior years, but for whatever reason, we absolutely treasured our ascension to the mountaintop, and I was there for that. In the moments after the victory, after I sought out my parents and brother in the stands, I stood in the locker room and soaked in champagne for a while, letting the smell overtake my senses. And before I hopped on the bus to the hotel around midnight, where the team was having a celebratory party for us, I sought out the Super Bowl trophy, put my hand on it and took a picture, basking in the knowledge I was making a memory that would last a lifetime.

Knowing that a bunch of us couldn't wait to go out on the town after, the team instructed us to leave our bags in front of our room and make sure we were back at the hotel by 9 a.m. the next morning so we could catch the bus to the airport. But they knew we were about to have a blast, so they also told us to just catch our own flight back to Indy if we missed the bus to the airport.

Man, we had a ball that night. The next morning, we had guys pulling up to the hotel at 7:30 a.m., 7:45 a.m. I'll never forget how one of my teammates still had his suit on, shirt buttoned halfway, tie barely hanging on, as he climbed aboard the bus, smiling like a madman, not even bothering to take a shower. And inside, I'm like, yo, we wouldn't have it any other way. The crazy thing was, as far as I know, everybody actually made the team flight!

When we got to Indianapolis—all of us were so wired that no one really slept on that plane ride, even though we'd been up all night—fans were waiting for us at the airport. That might have been one of the most welcoming experiences that I've had. I passed out when I got to my apartment, but woke up that evening after a power nap and went back out again with my teammates.

Now, I know it sounds like we celebrated a hell of a lot. And it's true, we did. But even at the age of 22, I knew that life is hard—I'd already had so many moments where I could have doubted myself or quit—so it is important to celebrate your biggest achievements, especially when you accomplish them in the face of adversity.

For me, winning Super Bowl XLI was the ultimate vindication, an "eff you" to everyone who made me feel like the underdog in the first place by doubting me. I'm sure many of my teammates, all of whom had to overcome something in their life to get to that moment, felt the same way. So, of course we enjoyed the hell out of it.

And you know what? I'll tell you one of the best parts about winning the Super Bowl: It's what we called the "Super Bowl Tour," the ensuing three months you spend celebrating throwing parties in everybody's hometown, all so the guys get to be called a "Super Bowl champion" in their respective cities.

After our Super Bowl parade in Indy, a bunch of us went to Las Vegas for the NBA's All-Star Weekend. It was my first time in Vegas and it was everything people said it was. And after that, it became a little competition between all of us to see who could throw the best party. Funny thing was, no matter where we were, people came out and showed us love. You know me and Cato June had to have a shindig in D.C. to celebrate, and a number of players came out. Robert Mathis had a party in Atlanta—he even set us up to get a police escort to the club—and if I may say, he pulled a smooth move with the police escort, trying to outshine me and Cato.

Philly, Puerto Rico … we were everywhere celebrating, so much so that when offseason workouts began in April and the offseason practices began in May, I couldn't believe how fast time had flown by.

Now came the next challenge, though, which was avoiding the sophomore slump in 2007. A lot of times, players come in, have a good year and surprise people, but for me, I didn't want to fall off and get written off as a fluke. I used that as motivation, which turned out to be all I needed, since that chip on my shoulder hadn't gotten any smaller. I went on to help the Colts to a 12-4 record as I was selected to my first Pro Bowl.

By the end of that second year, personally, things couldn't be going better for me. But I'm not going to lie—something was missing.

"All I need is a partner to play spades with the cards up/all trust"
Jay Z, *Excuse Me Miss*

A funny thing started happening to me in my second season. That year, when my teammates would be talking about their wives or significant others, I'd sometimes mention my college girlfriend.

"If I don't marry her," I told them, cynically, "I don't see myself getting married."

There was a reason for my iciness; by that point I'd seen and heard enough in the NFL to know that as a player, you're often a target. We're young men with means, and people are always looking for ways to exploit that, whether it's by robbing you or pulling you into bad business deals, or worse. I came to realize that you have to be careful who you let around you—my fifth rule for success.

Now, I felt pretty good about my core group of friends from back home—it's about 10-15 of us and maybe even more—and believe me,

I have the stories to prove their loyalty (which I'll share later this chapter). But the truth is, I always saw myself being with somebody that was there for me before the fame. Oftentimes athletes are targeted by some women, and it's not because of their personality, looks, morals, or values. Even mild-mannered Coach Dungy, a spiritual, religious man, had a saying: be careful of a female you don't know and you know too well. It meant that, while you obviously don't know the intentions of a stranger and should be wary, you should also be careful when dealing with a woman who knows you well, since she knows all your weak spots.

Although I was certainly enjoying the nightlife as a young starter on the Super Bowl champs, I knew I eventually wanted to settle down with a genuine woman, someone who would be my ride or die. My college girlfriend, I started to fully realize, was that. Hell, she liked me before I even became a good football player in college, let alone a Pro Bowl NFL safety. She was even there for me in a major way after one of my most eye-opening moments in life—when I got a DUI in college.

So yeah, I'll admit, starting in that second year, I began to think about her more and more. There was just one problem—we hadn't talked to each other in over a year.

When we won the Super Bowl, after I celebrated with my loved ones, I remember thinking, man, I wish she was here. Now don't get me wrong, the experience was cool because we had a great time and partied like crazy, but those are the moments you want to celebrate with the people who have been in your corner, and with her not being there, it was a little bittersweet, especially as I began to ponder the way she came through for me at Howard.

I originally bagged Samantha Romantini, a.k.a. Sam, off a box of Mike and Ike. That's my story and I'm sticking to it.

It was sophomore year at Howard, and me and my homeboys were walking on The Yard on a perfect Friday afternoon around lunchtime.

We spotted a short, nicely-built girl wearing heels and one of those hats you see ladies wearing at the Kentucky Derby.

"Damn, who's that!" one of the homies said.

"Yo, that's Sam," another said.

"For real? Damn!" another added.

Most of us knew Sam, because she was a helluva soccer player for Howard. Dudes would always talk about how bad she was, but I played it cool whenever I saw her, kept things real cordial.

But on this day, when I saw her, I was like "Yo, she's looking right." And only months later, when junior year rolled around, I put the full-court press on her, though it happened organically. It started with some small talk, as I'd chat her up while I stretched before football practice, right when Howard's soccer team—we all practiced on the same field—was wrapping theirs up.

One day that fall, I decided to invite her to a Saturday night party that me and three of my teammates were throwing off-campus after a home game, and she said she would come. Well, her friends ended up coming, but she didn't. So I couldn't wait to hit her with the guilt trip when I saw her next, but then she told me it was because of a death in her family. Aight, cool. Regardless, it gave us a chance for more dialogue, which set up our encounter nicely.

Days later, I was sitting on a couch in the football office when Sam walked in (the soccer and football teams shared office space, too). I was eating a box of Mike and Ike when I saw her. I'm still playfully guilt-tripping her for missing the party, you know, anything I can to keep the convo going.

Now, this is where she likes to act like she bagged me —instead of it being the other way around—but that's when she goes:

"Yo, let me get some of your Mike and Ikes," she said.

I gave her some, but I used it as a bartering chip to get her phone number first, and that's when we really hit it off. Soon after that, we went to the movies for our first date, and it wasn't long before we started spending quality time at my off-campus spot. We started hanging tough, and I quickly realized there was something different about her because I didn't mind being around her all the time. Unlike other times, it wasn't a situation where I'm with somebody for an hour or so and I'm already ready for her to leave.

So yeah, I knew it was really organic with Sam when I realized I could spend the whole day with her without getting bored or annoyed. I'd come to realize how much more she brought to the table in the spring of 2005, when I was forced to deal with one of the biggest mistakes of my young life.

We were supposed to just go home that night. Had we done that, everything would have been okay.

Alas.

It was a Saturday night in April 2005, just hours after me and my teammates had just wrapped up spring practice at Howard with our annual spring game. We were obviously all ready to celebrate the end of practice for a while, so we decided to go to an Alpha Kappa Alpha cabaret in Crystal City, Virginia.

We had a good time, and I'd had some drinks. I knew I was a little tipsy, but I definitely wasn't drunk, and besides, I figured getting a DUI was one of those things that would never happen to me. Still, me and my roommates aborted on our original plan to go to IHOP and decided to drive back to the house in D.C., at least until one of my roommates' girlfriend—who was at the cabaret that night—called and implored us to go to IHOP, where everybody had apparently gathered. So, we decided to turn around and head back.

Problem was, it was late at night, and if you've ever been on George Washington Memorial Parkway—where we were at the time—you know it's dark as hell and very few lights. We ended up missing the exit, and when I slowed down to read the next sign, I noticed a cop right there. I prayed he wouldn't pull out behind us, but no dice—next thing I knew, his red and blue lights were twirling behind us, and we were being pulled over.

So you know, I'm sobering up real quick. He asks if I've been drinking, and after I told him I had one or two, he had me get out of the car and do the sobriety test. I aced it, but I refused to blow into the breathalyzer on the spot, and because of that, he said he had to take me in to blow. I was under arrest.

By that point, our friends waiting at IHOP heard we had been pulled over, so they drove to where we were. There were also two other officers who drove up on the scene, and I'll never forget, prior to me taking the field test, one of them noticed how big my homeboys were and asked me if we played football.

"Yeah, we play football at Howard and we just had our spring game," I said.

"Man, you don't seem like you're intoxicated," he told me.

And after I nailed the field sobriety test, one of them asked who was in the car behind us, and I told them our friends from school.

"Well, we'll see if maybe we can get one of them to drive your car home and let you go," the officer said.

So he goes to talk to the officer that pulled me over, and I've got my fingers crossed, like man, please—give me this break. That's when both officers came back.

"Well, because he already started the paperwork, he can't stop doing the paperwork," one of them said.

So at that point, man, I'm like, it is what it is. They put me in the back of the cop car, and we start this two-hour odyssey where every police station we go to is closed. I'm thinking I've sobered up now for sure, and when we finally get to the station, two more cops I talked to said it didn't seem like I was intoxicated, giving me hope. I ended up blowing at the station and wouldn't you know it, I blew a 0.10.

And I'm like, damn, now I've got to deal with this shit. And the first thing I'm thinking is, I do *not* want my mom and dad to find out. I knew my parents were gonna flip out, especially my mom, for doing something so stupid and potentially harmful to myself.

Initially though, I thought I was going to get through it without telling them. I was 20 years old at the time, so they didn't need to be alerted.

And I'd hired a court-appointed lawyer on my own who actually did a nice argument reducing the consequences around the fact that I was a student and didn't have a job. I ended up getting a $100 fine. I also had to take five Alcoholics Anonymous classes and ten diversion courses, which I was to pay for of my own pocket.

I was pretty happy with that, but there was just one problem; the way the 10 diversion courses were spread out, I'd have to attend every Monday, starting in July and lasting through September. This posed a schedule issue, of course, because of football season. Thankfully, I even caught another break there, because they said I could double up on courses by taking two a week, allowing me to finish right before preseason camp.

But on those five Mondays where I had to attend two classes, it was hellish. This is when I knew Sam was down for me, because on those days, she picked me up at 6 a.m. every morning—remember, I couldn't drive then because of the DUI—and not only took me to the diversion courses, but waited on me to finish each day. And since I was uncomfortable going to the AA classes, she actually came and sat in those with me. I'm not gonna lie, that's when I knew she was the kind of woman for me, someone I could marry.

Because of Sam, I almost pulled it off without worrying my parents. But I didn't bank on the court sending my DUI paperwork to all my known addresses, even the one back home in Newport News.

That day, I felt my phone buzz. It was my mom, who I speak to every day, but she sounded nothing like the sweet lady who always lifted me up.

"I just got this paperwork!" she bellowed with anger. "A fucking DUI!"

As soon as she started cursing, I hung up. I said to myself, if she wants to continue this conversation, she's gonna have to make that 2-½ hour drive to D.C. to do it. We ended up talking again, of course, and after I told her how I'd already taken care of everything, she calmed down. She did, however, made it clear that she was upset that I kept it from them.

Even through all that, I still needed some other good people in my corner to make it through this unscathed. Like my second probation officer, who allowed me to leave D.C. to train in Atlanta for the NFL Draft if I promised to get her tickets whenever whichever team I landed with played the Falcons, her favorite team. Me being a man of my word, after I got drafted by the Colts, when we played the Falcons right before Thanksgiving in my second year, I made sure I got her some tickets.

As you might imagine, a tough situation like the DUI brought me and Sam closer together, which made it all the more disappointing when we broke up the next year. It was a miscommunication, and I'll take some of the blame. After I got drafted by the Colts, I wasn't sure if it was for the best if she moved to Indianapolis. I was only a sixth-round pick, and I was worried that if she moved there and I got cut, we'd both be assed out.

But that decision seemed to put some distance between us, and after a short visit at one point in my rookie year, we broke it off and lost contact with each other for several months, at least a year.

For as cruel as life can be, every once in a while, fate throws you an assist. That's what happened in January 2009, right after my third NFL season, when we ran into each other at a popular club in D.C. I remember sitting at a table with my homeboys when Sam, looking absolutely beautiful, bounced up the stairs. I couldn't do anything but smile and give her the biggest hug. We shared some small talk for a bit and she left, but she revealed she'd be in town for the rest of the week. I knew I couldn't let her slip away.

I had a plan, though. Jay Z, one of her favorite rappers, was having a concert in D.C. to celebrate the inauguration of our nation's first black president, Barack Obama, and I had four tickets. I initially told my homeboys they could come with me, but I knew this was my way back in with Sam. So I asked her to come to the show with me, and she brought her sister and a friend. My homeboys were pissed, but they understood what it was.

We went to the show, and man, we had a blast. We were vibing like the old days, and in my head I'm thinking, man, I miss her. Men always talk about having a female that can do everything—be a lady when it's time to be a lady, then be cool and hang out with the fellas—and she was that. We're at the show, and she's rapping the words to all the songs with me, and it felt like old times. I even had butterflies when I went to pick her up that night.

After the show, we went our separate ways, but after that, I was like, yo, I gotta have her back. So we started talking again, and that summer, I started floating the idea of her moving from New York—where she had a great life and a good job—to Indy. That was a big step for her and a big step for me—I had some things to learn about living with someone, as I apparently couldn't do some things I was accustomed to doing when I was a bachelor—but she moved in with me that summer and we've been together ever since.

In 2012, I proposed to her on her birthday—which fell on the bye week (how perfect was that?)—in a restaurant called Quality Meats. I flew out some of our friends and family, and I took her to a Jay Z concert in the Barclays Center in Brooklyn, which was fitting.

Our baby girl, Siani Loren Bethea, was born in 2013, right before Sam and I got married in 2014. Our son, Asiah "Ace" Bethea, was born two years later, and there's not a day that goes by that I don't remember that they're the reason I work so hard.

The truth is, whether you're a man or a woman, you need a loyal partner. Because during the good times, when everybody is happy to be around, they'll be tugging on you constantly. But when it's not so good, and things aren't going well for you, a lot of those people will fade to the back.

Since then, I can definitely say Sam has been a rock, a true partner. It helps that she was an athlete herself, so she gets how competitive I am and how I may need time to myself occasionally. Where some guys go home after practice and their wives throw the baby in their arms or some shit like that, Sam understands that I sometimes need some time to wind down after practice and let those competitive juices simmer. She's always there to keep me level-headed.

There's probably one good story that demonstrates how good Sam is at this. I remember in my second year, I had this defensive backs coach named Alan Williams, a man I call a good friend now, but damn if he didn't piss me off one day. Back then, I was still trying to prove I wasn't a fluke, and he took advantage of that by making sure he constantly asked me how much I weighed.

Now, I know this sounds like a small thing. But Coach would ask me that question once or twice a week, and if someone keeps asking you the same thing all the time—while you're doing everything you can to fix it—don't you think that would get annoying? Granted, I had a super-fast metabolism at the time, and I was drinking two or three protein shakes a day to keep my weight from dropping below 190, which was about 13 pounds below my weight at the NFL Combine. I even checked in constantly with the strength and conditioning coach to see if there was anything I could do to hold weight better, and he eventually settled on it being okay, since my play wasn't being affected.

But one day during a walkthrough in the middle of the 2007 season, Coach Williams asked me about it for the 2,333th time, and I snapped.

"Stop asking me about my damn weight," I yelled. "I'm getting tired of you asking about my damn weight!"

Now, I had a reputation as a pretty quiet guy at that point, so I could feel people staring at me in surprise. This was out of character for me, but at that point, I didn't care. Every time he asked me about my weight, it reminded me of my general lack of size—remember, I weighed 170 pounds coming out of high school—and how people had used that for years to doubt me.

Coach Williams and I laughed about it weeks later; blowups like that happen all the time in football, since you're dealing with ultra-competitive men under lots of pressure to perform. But when I got home that day, I was still pissed, and Sam—who was a master at reading my body language by that point—handled it like a pro.

"I'm getting tired of him asking me about my weight" I told her.

"Yeah, babe, that's weird," she replied.

After a while of back-and-forth, we eventually broke into laughter at the absurdity of it all. Looking back, it was an example of how having a loyal person around who knows you well can help defuse any negative situations.

Of course, while a man's world is often his family, I think when you're a guy, it's also important to keep plenty of guy friends around so they can call you on your bullshit and look out for you in situations when your family isn't present. And Lord knows, I've been in some dangerous situations where my core group of friends have come up huge.

"My brothers is my brother like my brother is"
Jay Z, *La Familia*

In the summer of 2014, I was hanging out in a club in Norfolk, Virginia, with my buddies L.A., Ish and Pac, guys who I go way back with. L.A. and I played high school football together, while I played against Ish and Pac.

I remember being in the club, having a good time, when the three of us started talking about how the bouncers really weren't doing a good job checking people at the door for weapons. We didn't think too much about it, though, at least until we started hearing gunshots ring throughout the club.

Pop! Pop! Pop!

I start ducking down when all of a sudden, my man Pac—dead serious—grabs me by the neck and chokeslams me to the ground while Ish jumped on top of me to protect me. We wait for the shots to calm down, and as soon as they stopped, we started hauling ass to the front door.

Much to my surprise, my man L.A. was outside already with the car, engine on, waiting for us to hop in and get the hell out of there. I have no idea how the hell L.A. got out of the club that fast and had the car waiting, but he did.

When we got in the car, we didn't even have to speak about what they did to look out for me. With real friends, shit like that can be left unsaid. They didn't do it because I was Antoine Bethea with the Indianapolis Colts, either—it was because we have genuine love for one another. If it was any other situation, I'd do the same for them. Like, if they were trying to drive drunk and I was sober, I'd say "Yo, give me your keys, I got it." There's just an unspoken bond, one that's reciprocal, and it's about the love we have for one another.

And trust me, while there's a group of 20 of us with like 20 years of friendship, there are no "yes men" in the crew. My boys are quick to tell me when I'm wrong.

"'Toine, you bullshittin'," they'll say.

"'Toine, you can't do that bro," they'll say.

I know that sounds like a lot of friends, though. Even when I bump into people from high school and they're like, who do you still talk to, I'll run down the names, they're like, "Whoa, all y'all are still friends?" and I'm like, "Yeah."

Between Carnell Williams, Gentry Parker, Ronald Coker, Reginald Blakeney, L.A., Geist, Lawrence White, Javie McIntyre, Pac, Tim Smith, Rod, Free, and more, I can tell you that I have some good guys in my corner.

Whether it comes to randomly checking in on my parents in Newport News when I'm not there or even grabbing my keys when I had too much to drink, I know I've got a group of hawk-eyed friends who always have my best interest at heart and keep a lookout for trouble.

That's important for anybody in any walk of life, but it's even more important for football players, just because there's so much danger or trouble lurking around every turn. There have definitely been times in my career where I've seen people mess up because they didn't have the right people in their corner.

Like, when I see guys being suspended for marijuana … I mean, everybody knows the process of drug testing. No true friend should be giving their homeboys a blunt that wants to see you succeed. You're supposed to be my man, right? We grew up together, right? We dreamt about this situation, right?

Granted, you're a grown-ass man and you're gonna do whatever the fuck you want to do. But we all make bad choices, and sometimes you need good people in your corner that can save you from yourself so nothing negative comes your way.

Now, don't get me wrong—at the end of the day, the responsibility for our behavior falls with ourselves, and I take an outrageous amount of pride in the fact that no one has to motivate me to be the best I can be—even Sam would tell you that. But once you've had some success in your chosen field, I'm not going to lie; often times, you find that your biggest opponent is yourself.

That's why it's just so important not to have a bunch of "yes men" around you. You need to be smart, diligent, even, about who you let in your corner, because the company you keep can not only offer protection against mistakes you unknowingly make, it's also a reflection of who you are. Character is everything, and the people you keep in your village as your confidants—not your constituents—should feed you just as much as you feed them in all sorts of areas: intellectually, emotionally, spiritually, professionally, etc.

I will say this, though; to make it in the league as long as I have—13 years—the responsibility of staying sharp falls on you. I've used plenty of tricks that help me stay sharp, which might be even harder than getting to the mountaintop in the first place.

Life will keep you on your toes, and I'd soon find that all it takes to learn the importance of keeping your edge is the resurfacing of a health issue to a loved one, in addition to the biggest defeat of your professional life, all in the same year.

RULE #6

Never Get Complacent

WHEN THE CLOCK STRUCK MIDNIGHT on January 1, 2009, I was convinced it would be the best year of my life. I was a 24-year-old former Pro Bowler entering my fourth professional season as a starter. And since I was on the last year of my rookie deal, I knew I stood to earn a contract within the next 15 months—either from the Colts or in free agency—that would change my life.

The way the month started—with me randomly bumping into Sam and rekindling a connection with the woman I saw myself marrying one day—gave me little reason to doubt my optimism. And neither did the retirement of Coach Dungy, the only head coach in the NFL I had ever known.

You see, I loved Coach—we all did—but most of us saw it coming. He'd been coaching for a few years while coping with the death of his son, and we'd all heard the whispers that the 2008 season would be it for him. We finished with a 12-4 record his final season, but I wish we sent him out better than a 23-17 loss to the San Diego Chargers in the wild card round.

And while the retirement of a beloved coach would typically sound alarm bells for a veteran locker room, it didn't in this case, since the Colts decided to promote his assistant head coach to the position. Coach Jim Caldwell was similar to Coach Dungy, and it goes beyond the fact they are both black. We all liked Coach Caldwell because of his cool and calm demeanor. He also relied on faith and had an ability to get his point across and command respect without yelling and screaming at us. He treated us like men, he was honest, and he kept his word. We'd all run through a wall for him.

Besides, we also knew that since Coach Caldwell had been there for so long, he wouldn't be making wholesale changes to the team like a new coach probably would. In our minds, we were one of the best teams in football, albeit one that had gotten a little unlucky in the playoffs in the two years since our Super Bowl win.

With Coach Caldwell around, we had no reason to think we wouldn't cement our legacy as one of the dynasties of the decade with another Super Bowl title. You see, we understood that the reason we performed well every year was that we were consistent about putting in the work. That was the ethos around the Colts back then, and honestly, I thank God every day I was drafted by that organization.

Hard work was never a problem for me, but thanks to the Colts' strong team culture, I grew tremendously as a player in Indianapolis, the place where I learned my sixth rule to success—never allowing complacency to set in.

Trust me, one thing I've learned over my 34 years on this earth is if you want to be successful at anything in life, you've got to have consistency. If you're married, you've got to be consistent with your spouse. If you have kids, you've got to consistently enforce rules if you want them to stick. And in my profession, you've got to be consistent with your production.

Consistency is the reason the Colts were able to develop so many diamond-in-the-rough players while Tony was there. In the NFL, players get better by being a *pro's* pro and approaching it more like a job and less like a game, at least until Sunday rolls around.

To be honest, this is something I learned through osmosis, just by being around successful, established players with long track records and watching what they did. Being in Indianapolis every day, you learn that guys like Peyton Manning, Marvin Harrison, Reggie Wayne, Jeff Saturday, Dwight Freeney, and Robert Mathis weren't All-Pros just because they were talented; they were All-Pros because they worked their asses off at it, constantly.

Seriously, these guys, they never took a day off from practice. And every time we were in meetings, they took notes. As a young player, I couldn't believe it. They basically approached it like rookies, even though all these guys were multi-time Pro Bowl players.

Take Reggie Wayne, for instance. He's one of the best receivers to ever play the game, and he catches balls for a living, right? During my second training camp with the Colts, I noticed that after every practice, he'd go to the Jugs machine and have somebody shoot balls out at him, and he'd catch the ball two-handed, one-handed, everything, all on his own volition. I wondered what he was doing at the time, thinking, damn, why is he doing that? But then, he'd go out in practice and catch balls one-handed, and in all sorts of crazy ways, and I realized he could do it because he practiced relentlessly.

By my fourth season—right before my contract year—I got to the point where I realized I might be able to accomplish some special things if I started doing what they did. Prior to that, I worked hard and trained hard, of course, but this was some next-level commitment stuff that went beyond simply playing balls out and doing what you were asked. I started working the Jugs machine, just like Reggie, and I also copied some of the personal body maintenance routines of Robert and Gary, since those guys' workouts had helped them stay on the field consistently. That meant daily sessions in the cold tub, plus pilates, stretches, and a personal chef; not to mention twice-a-week massages and weightlifting sessions three or four times a week.

I feel like most people know the importance of consistency when you're working toward a goal, but the hard truth is, it takes mental toughness to do things anyway when you don't feel like it. The realest thing I ever heard was, "if it was easy, everybody would do it." When football gets hard and I don't feel like working out, I tell myself that all the time. And I'm pretty sure you can apply that to anything in your life.

For instance, say the average person wants to lose weight, but they don't have the time or the means to achieve that. I get that. Well, there's *something* they can do, and most of the time, people internally know that. The problem is making the sacrifice and putting in the necessary work to do it.

I don't want you to feel like I'm preaching to you or anything, because I've been there. There are lots of times I don't feel like working out. But I just tell myself that someone else is out there putting in the work, maybe a hungry young cat coming to take my job. If working out was easy, the gym would be packed. But it's a mindset. You have to tell yourself you're an anomaly, and that it's because you work out when you don't feel like it that you're able to succeed when others fail.

That said, I couldn't have been prouder in 2009, when I took my training and discipline to the next level and proceeded to make 95 tackles, five pass deflections, and four interceptions on the way to earning my second Pro Bowl nod. To me, that not only proved I wasn't a fluke, it also showed that I was starting to—finally—get a little respect at this point. When people were talking about some of the top safeties in the league, my name was being mentioned, and after spending my entire career as an underdog, you know that felt good.

What's more, we'd had a great season under Coach Caldwell in his first year, going 14-2 and reaching the Super Bowl again for the second time in four seasons. And at this time, I'm not going to lie—I felt like, man, I'm having a great career. In four years, I'd made two Pro Bowls, earned a championship ring, and was playing for Super Bowl win No. 2. I don't think you can write up the beginning of a career too much better than that, unless there's an MVP or an All-Pro selection in there.

On the real, the fact that the Super Bowl was being held in Miami, the city where we won it all just three years prior, only added to my confidence in getting my second ring. I'd said 2009 was going to be my year, and lo and behold, we were about play for a championship in the same place we'd done it already. It must be destiny, I thought.

But as I keep saying, life will humble you. And as confident as I was, I knew better than to take anything for granted. The phone call I received in April 2009, just 10 months prior to the Super Bowl I was about to play, jilted me to that reality.

Throughout offseason practices in May 2009, my teammates were busting my chops. My entire life, I'd rocked a short, close haircut, so when I decided to shave all my hair off and go bald, they would not stop making jokes. I laughed along, because in a pro locker room, you never show weakness by taking good-natured stuff like that too personally.

But they didn't know why I'd really decided to shave my hair. See, that month, my mom had to shave her hair off because she was about to undergo surgery for a brain aneurysm. We'd found out in April, during one of the regular checkups she's always had to have since she survived the brain tumor when I was eight years old. I knew about it almost immediately, since me and my mom talk damn near every day.

She explained that the doctors had long known about the aneurysm, even back when they detected the tumor, but because it was so small—and because she was already having major surgery to remove the tumor—they didn't want to risk it then. But now, 17 years later, the bill had come due. The doctors said it had only grown over the years, likely from stress and old age, and the only alternative to keep it from growing further was to cut into her skull and clamp it.

This was a scary deal, since the aneurysm was actually closer to her brain than the tumor was, and you hear about people dying from aneurysms every single day. So of course, I wanted to skip parts of the offseason practices to fly home for the surgery, which would be done in May. But my mom, knowing that it was a contract year for me, insisted I stay in Indianapolis and take care of my business. I couldn't believe it.

"Baby, you don't have to come back," she reassured me, before I politely told her she must be out of her mind. "I want you to stay and do what you do. As time's gone by, God's been on our side."

Now inside, I'm like, shit, I only got one mom, so you can say all you want, but I'm there. But she insisted I stay in Indianapolis and practice. Even my mom understands the old saying of the NFL standing for "Not For Long."

So I listened to her out of respect, and I was grateful to hear her 4½-hour surgery went well. But I did fly back and see her as soon as I could, and when offseason practices ended in June, I flew back to Newport News to spend an extended amount of time at home just so I could help look out for her when the hospital finally released her.

I'm glad I did. It wasn't long after that I noticed she was breathing really heavily around the house, and while she tried to be strong and blow it off—"I'm just out of shape," she kept saying—I knew that type of heavy breathing wasn't simply lack of stamina. She was gasping for air more than anything.

I remained steadfast in that conviction, even after we took her back to the hospital and they diagnosed her with something that didn't seem serious enough, considering how bad she sounded. When we got home and things didn't get better, we took her back and that's when the doctors—who ran some more tests—saw she had blood clots in her lungs.

As you can imagine, I was so pissed about the earlier misdiagnosis. Fortunately, the blood clot issue was fixable and it didn't require surgery, but it was just another challenge for my mom, who soon found herself on more meds, including blood thinners. Since I was home at the time, I regularly took her to her appointments during the day and stayed on her about taking her medicine. She still wasn't 100 percent by the time I left for training camp in mid-July, but by October or so, she was fine.

I went on to have one of my best seasons that year. While my improved, Colts-approved focus on intense, consistent preparation—not to mention the reality that I was playing for my next contract—played a large role in that, so did the toughness my mom showed that year. She was to demonstrate more Mom Dukes tenacity in 2015, when she was diagnosed with—and beat—breast cancer.

Her latest scare made four significant medical issues (a brain tumor, brain aneurysm, blood clots in her lungs, and breast cancer) that she attacked and conquered with an amazing spirit. Through it all, she rarely complained. She always kept battling, consistently showing mental toughness that we admired. I channeled her strength when I faced whatever little injuries I did on the field as I proceeded to start 119 straight games in the NFL.

So yes, if there was any part of me that wanted to slide to complacency in 2009, when my mom dealt with the aneurysm, it simply wasn't happening that year. And as we continued to roll through regular season and the playoffs, there was only one way I wanted it all to end—with another championship.

I stood on the sideline in disbelief, watching No. 22 in a white jersey streak untouched into the end zone as Saints fans went wild.

"Damn," I said with disgust.

This was February 7, 2010, the fourth quarter of showdown against the New Orleans Saints in Super Bowl XLIV, and I could barely believe what I saw. Tracy Porter, the Saints' second-year cornerback, had just intercepted Peyton Manning—a future Hall of Famer—for a 74-yard pick-6 that put us in a 31-17 hole with 3 minutes, 12 seconds left to play.

And, I'm not going to lie; that was the moment where I knew we were in deep trouble that night. So much so that even to this day, when they show that clip on television, I'm like, "Shit." But I never turn away; by now, you guys know how big I am on finding motivation everywhere. As hard as it is to swallow, I get pissed—and ready to start working—every time I see it.

The Saints went on to win by that same score, and for everyone else other than us, it was a heartwarming story. Everybody knew about the way Hurricane Katrina destroyed New Orleans, and for them to come back and win the Super Bowl only five years later, it felt like everyone was happy for them.

But for us, it was just misery. No one really cared to see us win again, other than Colts fans, but we were really looking forward to winning and tearing the city up that night, just like we did the last time. I would have been a little more subdued, now that I was three years older and Sam was there—we had been rocking together for nearly a year now, and she sat near my parents and brother during the game. I really wanted her to experience what it's like to win the Super Bowl, but obviously, it didn't go down that way.

For as amazing as you feel when you win the Super Bowl, you feel just as bad when you lose. It was kind of surreal, to be honest, being on the other side of it. Instead of walking off the field like a conquering hero, you're thinking man, let's hurry up and get out of here. Instead of smiles, loud laughter and an abundance of champagne in the locker room, all you see are frowns, tears, and grown men speaking in quiet, hushed tones, silently wanting to finish their media interviews, take their showers and get on the bus.

And a Super Bowl loss doesn't just hurt the players, coaches, and front office members, either. From the top down, so many band together to make the machine that is an NFL football team run smoothly. From the cooks, to the equipment guys, to the janitors, to the scouts, everybody is doing their job in hopes of the team prevailing during this one moment, when you play 60 minutes to win a title. And for us not to get it done, everybody's hurt.

Hell, even the ride back to the hotel was different, and it's kind of depressing, to be honest. You play all those games—at least 23, dating back to the preseason—and put in all the work, only to fall *one game shy*. It hurts, especially when you compare it to the previous time we were there, when we owned Club Force and felt like the Kings of Miami.

This time, the guys who didn't just go back to their rooms gathered at the hotel bar for some drinks before retiring for the night. That's how deflating it was, and to me, it showed how much we cared. Easily, some player who really didn't care could have went out and partied on the low that night. But as far as I know, no one went out that night.

It was a pretty miserable way to head into the offseason, and the feeling of redemption—of getting back to the Super Bowl and winning—is one I've chased ever since. It's a big reason I've been able to stay in such good shape and play for 13 years. Every time I think about it, it pisses me off...which means I get up and bust my ass.

But at the moment, I also had other matters to tend to, namely my contract situation. Normally, after completing my rookie deal, I would be getting ready to be an unrestricted free agent, but with the collective bargaining agreement set to expire, the NFL was heading toward an uncapped year, which meant I needed six years of experience to be unrestricted, as opposed to the typical four.

Yet, even though I decided to skip the first few months of offseason practices—a typical strategy for players seeking new deals—I remained pretty optimistic that everything was going to work out. I was still young, just 26, and I'd been one of the Colts' most consistent starters. Plus, I wanted to stay in Indy anyway, even though I couldn't test the market because of the lockout and the Colts technically could have forced me to play on the $2.5 million restricted tender.

So when Adisa told me the Colts were prepared to do right by me, and ultimately ended up offering an extension, I was obviously thrilled. I thought, damn, that shows how much they value me, because they didn't have to do that during the lockout year. And I was one of only a handful of extensions that got done across the league during the lockout, so there's definitely some truth to that.

I'll never forget the day my agent, Asida Bakari, got the call from the Colts, locking the deal down with the final numbers. We were working out together at a YMCA in Washington, D.C., when he got the call from the Colts. After stepping away for a few minutes, he turned to me.

"They're offering you a four-year deal worth $27 million," he told me. "Are you good with this?"

Hell yeah, I was good with it. If I was a free agent, maybe I could have played teams off each other and gotten more. But I'm not a greedy guy, and I took the deal. For one, it was more money than anyone in my family had ever seen. And two, I'd learned long before that tomorrow isn't promised—a lesson that had just been reinforced a year earlier by my mom's unexpected new health issues.

As soon as we finalized it, I called my family and told them the good news. But you know what's funny? Even though I was richer than I ever could have imagined, the chip on my shoulder was still pretty big. Maybe I wasn't a 12 on the motivational scale of 1-to-10 anymore, but I was definitely a nine still. I didn't come from money, I was alright without money, and I wasn't going to let money change me. For me, it was just the icing on the cake of all the hard work I put in.

But if I wasn't the best safety in the league—and I never thought I was—then I knew I still had work to do. And inside, there was definitely a part of me that was scared of bombing out or looking like a big-money bust—I didn't want to be the guy who disappeared after signing a big deal. The Colts showed faith in me, so it was now on me to uphold my end of the bargain in 2010 and beyond.

"Determined to be the best, not lookin' back at regrets/How many people you bless is how you measure your success"
Rick Ross, *Shot To The Heart*

When people know you make a lot of money, it turns out, a lot of business opportunities come your way, whether they're good or bad. Let's just say there's a lot of friends with business ideas. A lot.

It's one of those things where you have to get a good, solid group behind you, whether it's lawyers or financial people, and let them skim through everything and do the due diligence to protect your assets.

One of the first things I did after signing my deal was start the Antoine Bethea Safe Coverage Foundation, a nonprofit with the mission to provide access and resources to students in my hometown in hopes of helping them further their education. I always said when I was in a position to give back, I would. So my foundation not only pays for high school kids who have never been out of Newport News to tour Virginia and D.C. colleges like Howard, George Mason and Georgetown, but also awards them some money.

The nonprofit was born out of my past experiences. I had some high school friends that wanted to go to college but didn't have the resources, and I know I was lucky my parents were able to take it on the chin my freshman year at Howard and pay my tuition until I earned a full ride.

But the thing I was most proud of that I was able to do around the time I got my contract was finish my degree at Howard. A month before I got my new deal, I walked across the stage at Howard with my criminal justice degree. I went back because I promised my mother I would, back when I left school a semester early to start preparing for the draft, so right after the Super Bowl loss—and knowing I'd probably be holding out from the Colts for a while—I enrolled in school and started attending the five classes I needed to pass to get my degree. I don't know if it was because I was a little older or what, but going to class and learning was actually pretty fun. I retained the information from class easier, and studying was easier, too.

One thing that was good about the experience was that it taught me that I definitely wasn't ready to retire. Your days in the NFL are so structured—everything is laid out for you—that when you don't have that anymore, you're like, damn, what do I do now? For those four months I was back in school, I worked out in the morning with a personal trainer, went to class, went home and studied and then had the rest of my afternoon to do whatever I wanted. It would have been easier if Sam was with me, but she decided to go to school in Miami to start working on being a financial advisor. She's not doing that now—when we had little mama in 2013, life just got in the way—but I'm still proud of her for embracing that challenge.

I returned to the Colts that summer as a new college graduate, and a well-paid one, at that. But there was no time to rest, as all of us were determined to erase the miserable taste the Super Bowl loss left in our mouths.

I ended up having a strong season, recording a career-high 106 tackles with five pass deflections and an interception, but while we again made the playoffs and won the AFC South for the ninth straight year, it marked the first time since 2002 we didn't win at least 12 games, and we lost at home in the wild card round to the New York Jets 17-16.

None of us knew it at the time, but that season would essentially be the swan song for the Peyton Manning - Tony Dungy era. The season that followed, it turns out, would be the toughest of my professional life, but it's one that helped me build character, as I quickly learned that losing would be the ultimate test of my sixth rule of success.

When we reported for training camp in July 2011, we had many of the same players that were key cogs in our tremendous run—Reggie Wayne, Dallas Clark, Jeff Saturday, Gary Brackett, Robert Mathis, Dwight Freeney, and myself.

But one key player was missing, and it was a massive one: Peyton. He'd been having trouble with his neck, and while there always seemed to be optimism about his ability to suit up when the season rolled around, when we got a chance to watch him throw, it was clear he wasn't the same. Peyton never had the strongest arm anyway—it wasn't like he was John Elway—but with his neck injury (he needed spinal fusion surgery, turns out) the ball was just dying out of his hand.

As such, when the regular season rolled around, and the club announced he'd miss the opener against Houston—ending his consecutive starts streak at 208 games—and likely much more, I just don't think we were prepared for that. We just assumed he'd be there when the games mattered, like he always was.

But he wasn't, even though we know he would have killed to be out there with us. With Peyton on the shelf, the team paid veteran Kerry Collins $4 million to come out of retirement a few weeks before the season and give us a fighting chance on a week-to-week basis, but Kerry only played in three games that year due to a concussion, and the other guys we had that year—Curtis Painter and Dan Orlovsky—struggled.

As a result, our offense was awful that year (30th) and our pass defense—which allowed a ridiculous 71.2 completion percentage to opposing quarterbacks—was, too. We lost our first 13 games before mercifully ending the "winless season" talk by beating the Titans 27-13 in Week 15.

Through all that, though, I felt compelled to show my mental toughness every day by doing my job. I wanted people to know that I was going to bring my lunch pail every day, and whether things are going good, bad or whatever, you can count on No. 41 to come and work. The coaches started using me around the line of scrimmage more to help our run defense, and I ended up setting a career-high in tackles with 139—I think they shorted me out of some, too.

We ended up finishing 2-14, and Coach Caldwell ended up getting fired, which I didn't think was fair, though you can argue it was a decision that needed to be made. The same can be said for the team's ensuing decision to trade Peyton to the Broncos and draft Andrew Luck No. 1 overall. People were talking about Luck being the next Peyton, and sure, when you run a business, you've got to make tough decisions like that. But I'm not going to lie—when both those moves were made, it was tough for the holdovers to swallow. That's when I knew this league was ruthless for real, because if anyone should have retired an Indianapolis Colt, it was Peyton Manning.

Slowly but surely, the culture that Coach Dungy and Coach Caldwell had fostered during their combined 10-year tenure as head coach faded as the core players who carried out the "no excuses, no explanation" ethos of hard work and no complacency either retired or simply moved on.

I would eventually fall into the latter category, unfortunately.

I saw it through with the Colts for the next two seasons, starting all 16 games each year and averaging 105 tackles, and we had some good times, too, as Luck turned out to be the real deal. We went to the playoffs both seasons, going a combined 22-10 in the regular season and even winning a playoff game in 2013, when we mounted the second-largest comeback in NFL playoff history.

But that was the last year of my contract, and after the Colts' new regime had brought in some of their own guys in the secondary they wanted to pay—like safety LaRon Landry and cornerback Vontae Davis—I figured I'd be playing elsewhere in 2014, since teams aren't going to pay three defensive backs big money because of the salary cap.

However, the way my separation with the Colts went down simply didn't sit right with me, and only made it easier not to get complacent. The general manager at the time was Ryan Grigson, and Adisa told me he wouldn't even answer his calls when he tried to talk to him about an extension for me. Every time, he'd put an underling on the phone with him who apparently told him they felt my play was diminishing because I'd be turning 30 before the next season.

I never heard from Grigson, either, for the record, and I felt like after everything I'd done for the franchise in my eight years there—like starting 123 of 128 games, going to two Pro Bowls, and helping secure the franchise's first title, all while doing a lot in the community and never being an off-the-field headache—I deserved a little more respect than that. Had he just called me and said "Okay 'Toine, we're gonna go another route," I could have respected that. But we didn't hear anything from him, and that left a sour taste in my mouth for a while.

When I hit the free agent market in March 2014, it was the first time in years I was unemployed, but it was also the first time I was able to shop my wares on the market. Because I had been so productive the previous year, I was confident I would get picked up. I still I had a lot of good ball left in me, and at least two good teams—San Francisco and Green Bay—agreed, as both expressed interest in signing me.

San Francisco had been to a Super Bowl more recently than Green Bay had been (2012 compared to 2010) and when I saw the talent they had on their defense—guys like Justin Smith, Aldon Smith, Patrick

Willis, NaVorro Bowman, and Ray McDonald—I realized I had never played behind cats like that.

Plus, I'd heard some great things about the defensive coordinator, Vic Fangio, and when I paid a visit and the money was right—four years, $21 million—I signed on the dotted line, ready to show the Colts what they were missing and prove to the world I wasn't washed up or anything.

Turns out, my tenure in San Francisco didn't go the way I planned, at least when it came to team success. But it was there that I came to realize my final rule to success, one that I'm most proud of enacting because it remains a controversial stance to this day.

RULE #7

Stand For What You Believe In

AFTER BEING LET GO BY the Indianapolis Colts, my motivation—on a scale of 1-10—went back to a 12. I was also excited to go to a team with Super Bowl aspirations, the direction I believed the 49ers were headed in ... at least until I got there and saw how things were being handled.

Now, there was a lot of talk in the media about the strained relationship between the head coach, Jim Harbaugh, and the general manager, Trent Baalke. I can't tell you if it was true or not but something was wrong. That was my first time really dealing with that in the NFL, since the Colts ran so smoothly under Bill Polian for all those years I was there.

And let me tell you something, the players in San Francisco could tell something was off. The machine that is an NFL team is so massive, so complex, that when you have a riff—when two people don't see eye-to-eye on how to win games and aren't communicating properly—it's gonna trickle down, and people are going to notice. Players are grown men, and we're smart enough to tell the organization isn't moving in a positive direction. That's how a team with as much talent as we had ends up going 8-8, as we did in 2014, my first year in the Bay Area.

That being said, I'm not really sure who was to blame for all the dysfunction. All I knew is that I respected Coach Harbaugh, and for all you hear about how different or eccentric he is, my interactions with him were pretty good. He was all about hard work, he was fanatical about winning games, which he did plenty. That one year I played for him, you can tell it bothered him we weren't as good as we all thought we should be. We had a veteran locker room full of guys that were itching to get back to the Super Bowl, and it bothered all of us, really.

I do think Coach Harbaugh treated veterans with respect, which was something I appreciated and saw right off the bat. I'd gotten a concussion in our preseason opener against Denver—I was hit in the head by receiver Cody Latimer when he was trying to block me and suffered my first documented concussion—and we all decided I should sit for the rest of the preseason. As a 30-year-old, eight-year vet, I was good with that and thought that would be the smartest decision, since I needed to be full strength for the regular season so I could help lead a secondary that had lost three starters from the previous season.

However, I wondered if that was really okay, at least in the minutes after our last preseason game against Houston, when we were standing in the locker and Coach Harbaugh started to deliver his postgame message to us.

"Alright, preseason is over, we're gonna have our cuts, we're about to get ready for real football," he told us. "Nobody gets hurt in the preseason, let's go."

So now, here I am, an injured guy in the locker room, and I sense everybody looking at me, because I sure as shit had gotten hurt. So I decided to have some fun with the moment while also testing Coach Harbaugh a bit.

"Hold on, hold up!" I half-jokingly yelled at Coach Harbaugh. "What you trying to say?"

I laughed inside when he immediately realized he'd messed up.

"No, no, no, 'Toine, I didn't mean like that," he said.

When we got on the plane to San Francisco later that evening, I was sitting in first class with the rest of the vets when Coach walks up there and kneels beside me.

"Hey, man," he said, "I didn't mean anything by that."

I appreciated the gesture, and by then, I was ready to let him in on the joke.

"Nah, man, I was just messing with you," I told him. "I knew what you were trying to say."

"I just wanted to make sure we're good," he repeated.

We were. After that, Coach Harbaugh was good with me. I returned in time for the season opener and proceeded to play nearly every defensive snap and record 86 tackles, 10 pass deflections and four interceptions on a top-five defense. We had some other dogs on D that year—including All-Pro types like Patrick Willis and Justin Smith—so I take tremendous pride in being named the 49ers' Team MVP in 2014 and earning the third Pro Bowl nod of my career.

In retrospect, that was without a doubt a great year for me. Not only did I show everyone I still had it, but remember, in June of that year, I got married to my best friend and long-time girlfriend in D.C., which was an amazing moment for both of us.

Turns out that would be the only time during my three-year stint with the 49ers that we would even come close to finishing .500, though the rest of my tenure would still prove fruitful as I managed to cement my seventh and final rule for success—stand for what you believe in—thanks in large part to quarterback Colin Kaepernick.

"Time to remind me I'm black again, huh? All this talking back,
I'm too arrogant, huh?"
Jay Z, *Nice*

When I first got to San Francisco, Kaepernick was a legit star after taking the 49ers to the Super Bowl in 2012. A 6-foot-4, 230-pound dual threat with terrific athleticism and a rocket arm, Coach Harbaugh knew how to stress defenses with Kaep's multitude of skills.

But for all his celebrity, Kaep was a guy who pretty much kept to himself for the most part. Don't get me wrong—he spoke to us and he was cool, but he wasn't a rah-rah type of guy. He was reserved, but a cool dude who was liked in the locker room. At the time, there was certainly no way to know he'd lead a revolution of sorts.

However, once Coach Harbaugh left to coach the University of Michigan and the front office decided to hire from within by promoting defensive line coach Jim Tomsula to the position, Kaep's fortunes—and the fortunes of the team—changed quickly. While the offense struggled for the second year in a row, finishing 30th in total yards, the defense—which had a new defensive coordinator now that Coach Fangio had left for the Bears—plummeted from No. 5 in 2014 to No. 29 in 2015.

It was even a tough year for me, as I had my streak of 119 consecutive starts snapped by a torn pec muscle that caused me to miss nine games. In the end, it was a disaster of a 5-11 season that led Coach Tomsula—a good dude and a good d-line coach who just wasn't ready to be a head coach—to get fired.

The team decided to hire Chip Kelly, an offensive guru who did big things at the University of Oregon, and the thought was that he could bring the best out of a dual-threat quarterback like Kaepernick, who completed 59 percent of his passes for 1,615 yards, six touchdowns and five interceptions in only nine games in 2015.

Coach Kelly had a reputation, though. After going 10-6 in his first two years as the Philadelphia Eagles' head coach, he was fired after a 7-9 campaign in 2015, and there were some comments from some of the black players there that he took offense to black players with opinions. He traded away some opinionated guys, like star running back LeSean McCoy, and ex-players kept hinting in the media at how uncomfortable he was around black players. I also don't think it helped that he kept receiver Riley Cooper around after he was caught on camera using the N-word.

But I've got to say, all my dealings with Coach Kelly were good. Granted, I don't have beef with many people because I don't ask for much—just be a man of your word, do your job, and follow through on what you say you're going to do—but as soon as he was hired, he was open about what happened in Philly, explaining that he thought he got a bad rap because guys sometimes have a difficult time adjusting when a new regime takes over. I'd found that to be true during my years in the league, so I decided to give him the benefit of the doubt and form my own opinion.

Everyone thought that might be the major storyline for us that season, but little did anyone know our quarterback was about to steal the show by elevating the conversation about a major problem in this country that was previously unrecognized by the majority of Americans.

Around the Fourth of July in 2016, I was in Miami for the yearly retreat my agent, Adisa Bakari, puts on for his players. Kaep and me were just chilling, talking about the latest news in the world. Philando Castile, a 32-year-old unarmed black man, had just been shot by a police officer during a routine traffic stop, and both Kaep and I were flabbergasted.

"We've got to do something about this," Kaep told me. "Something's got to change."

He asked me what I thought about it, and I agreed with him. But I didn't know he was going to do what he decided to do, which was to sit during the National Anthem. None of us did; aside from that conversation we had in July, it came out of the blue.

Although he'd sat during the anthem at least one other time that preseason (against Denver), it really blew up after he sat during the anthem prior to our preseason finale against Green Bay, when he talked to NFL.com reporter Steve Wyche—a proud Howard grad, like me—about the reasons why he was doing it.

And contrary to what people may tell you, the reasons why he was protesting were very, very clear. In the wake of the shooting of Castile, who was just the latest unarmed African-American to die at the hands of police, Kaepernick wanted to bring attention to the problems of police brutality and social injustice against people of color. That's it. And personally, I completely understood, 1,000 percent. After all, as an

African-American male in America, I've been profiled and harassed by police before, and my friends have, too.

Once Kaep started protesting, it stirred up memories of the past for all of us, all of which led me to ponder a simple question after the game—would I stay neutral and not protest, absolving myself of the blowback that had already started to surround Kaep? Or would I sit with him during the anthem before the next game and bear some of that burden, potentially putting my football livelihood at risk by contributing to the possible "distraction" football organizations hate?

In essence, I had to ask myself: could I look myself in the mirror if I didn't speak up for my people? To answer that question, I had to search within myself and dive into my own past.

The first incident happened when I around 26 years old. I was driving around my neighborhood in Newport News when a cop pulled me over in my black Cadillac Escalade—which featured nice rims and tinted windows—and said I evaded a red traffic light.

Problem was, I knew for a fact that I didn't. I'd lived there for 14 years by then, so I knew the lay of the land and where all the lights were. There wasn't a light in the vicinity. Trust me on that. Nevertheless, I was eventually surrounded by six police cars, hands on weapons before they let me go.

Six. Police. Cars. For allegedly evading a traffic light. Really?

The second time also happened back in my 20s, when I told some of my best friends from Newport News to go to my parents' house and grab the Escalade, so they could drive up to D.C. and hang out with me for the weekend. They came up and had a great time, but on their way back to Virginia, they got pulled over on the interstate because—the police admitted to them—they suspected the car for drug activity.

Which couldn't have been further from the truth. My friends showed them the registration and everything for the car with my name on it, and they told the officers that they knew me. But the police still made them get out of the car as they proceeded to tear it up. They were searching for drugs, obviously, ripping through the glove compartment, the trunk, everything,

Eventually, they hopped in their cop car and left without straightening up the mess they made.

"Y'all drive safe," is all one of them said afterward.

When my homeboys called me after they drove off and told me what went down, I was pissed. But I was also grateful that's all that happened. Situations like these are what make some people of color mistrust the police. And I wish that was the worst example I have.

Not too long ago, I bought my new Audi R8, and it had just been delivered to my local dealership in Newport News. I had the plates I needed to put on the car, but I didn't have the screws to put them on, so I drove it to my parents' house and put the plates in my front windshield, figuring I'd be fine if a cop stopped me for driving without plates. But still, I asked my dad to follow, just in case, because I know that driving with no plates is just asking for trouble.

Suddenly, as we're heading to the store to get the screws, a regular-looking car whizzes past me, then slows down. I pass them up, figuring it was some dumb kid, when they did it again. And I see another regular-looking car pull up to the side of my father, waving at him to back off.

Another car slides up behind me, and suddenly I'm surrounded by at least three unmarked police cars. It was the "jump out boys", the Newport News slang for undercover narcs. I was laughing at the ridiculousness of this all—me, a drug dealer? Please—until I noticed that they had their hands on their guns as they slowly got out of their cars.

So they walk over to my car, and they're flashing a bright-ass light inside. I roll my window down, and they ask my name.

"Antoine—Antoine Bethea," I said.

"We had reports this car is stolen," the officer said.

That was a lie, clearly, because I had literally just gotten it off the dealer's lot.

"No, it's not," I said, annoyed.

"What do you do for a living?" he asked.

I felt the anger rising within now, and it didn't take long for it to start bubbling to the surface.

"Why does that matter?" I responded angrily.

Now, this was stupid. You never know how these types of situations go, and I shouldn't have been saying some smart shit like that to cops, because at any moment that entire situation could have taken a turn for the worst. I don't make excuses—you know that about me—but that's how angry I was that these guys were lying on me, that I'd put myself in danger by talking back like that.

My point is, when you deal with cops and they're treating you unfairly, your anger can exceed the point of self-control. My pops can testify to that, because he was still nearby—damn I'm glad he tagged along, in retrospect—and he was going absolutely crazy. By that point, he'd transitioned from the Army to a deputy sheriff position in the Newport News police department, and he was walking around yelling, demanding every one of their badge numbers.

Eventually, one of the cops looked at my license and recognized my name and who I was, and he ended up letting me go. But oftentimes, I think about what would have happened if my dad wasn't there, or what would have happened if he wasn't a deputy sheriff or if that one cop didn't recognize my name.

Sometimes, I think about all the innocent young brothers and sisters that get pulled over by cops all the time in situations just like that and aren't a celebrity or public figure. What happens to them? Every once in a while, they end up like Philando Castile, Eric Garner, Terence Crutcher, Sandra Bland, Tamir Rice, Alton Sterling, Freddie Gray, and so many more.

Now, I don't say all this to intimate that all cops are bad. Quite the contrary. They are needed. But it was right then, in the week after Kaep's story became national news, that I realized I couldn't live with myself if I didn't protest. I went to an HBCU, after all, and the whole time I was there, we were taught to always speak up for our community. As a leader and a proud black man with a platform, I felt it was my responsibility to speak up for those without a voice.

But how would I protest? Kaep eventually shifted from sitting to kneeling during the anthem, which he did because he didn't want to offend veterans who served our country and fought in wars. I thought about joining him during our season opener against the Rams—which was scheduled for September 12, 2016, one day after 9-11—but after talking to my dad, a veteran who retired as a sergeant first class in the Army, I changed my mind.

My parents understood what the protest was about, and he made it clear that whatever choice I made, there would be some who didn't like it. He thought it was important for me to consider the way some in the military might feel about kneeling, and since I grew up in an area with a heavy military presence, I had a lot of conversations with people who did support some form of protest during the anthem and a lot of people who didn't.

However, my dad was definitely on board with me doing something, and so were my mom and my brother.

"Because after you retire," Pops said, "you're still gonna be a black man."

My father was right, of course. Of course he was. At the end of the day, I raised my right fist (a long-understood black power symbol) during the anthem. Not everybody would agree or accept that gesture.

Once I started protesting, some NFL fans started sending American flags addressed to me at the practice facility with notes saying, "If you don't like X, Y, and Z, get out of the country." It was just your typical nonsense from people who don't have to worry about the day-to-day issues that some African-Americans encounter.

These are the people who keep telling us to "respect the flag," who act like they don't know why we're protesting, and it really frustrates me. I truly believe that people know exactly what the protests are really about, but they're not conscious enough to talk about the issues at hand because police brutality and social injustice do not affect them directly. Thus, they willfully lack the empathy to understand our cause, and honestly, it's sad.

As such, I used it as motivation, but I didn't lose any sleep over it. By standing up for what I believed in and joining Kaep, Eric Reid, and Eli Harold (who kneeled), it gave me a sense of purpose, a sense that my life was about more than just what I wanted or needed. Truly winning in life means affecting more lives than just your own, and in my book, that makes guys like Kaep and Eric Reid real winners.

As for Kaep, you already know how I feel about him. He can still play in this league, but in exchange for his career, his cause has enlightened scores of people, and that's exactly what he wanted. His willingness to kneel has sparked uncomfortable conversations about injustice and oppression of people of color, and to be honest, it feels good to know I played a small role in that.

Although I look back fondly on the stance we took in an effort to bring awareness to an important cause for African-Americans, when it comes to the 2016 season, that's about the only positive thing I can say about that season.

Coach Kelly decided to start Blaine Gabbert over Kaep to start the year, and while Kaep eventually worked his way into the mix—completing 59 percent of his passes for 16 touchdowns and four interceptions—we were awful, going 2-14. That cost Coach Kelly—who I came to like and still stay in contact with to this day—his job, and the same goes for Baalke.

For the record, while there were some people in the locker room that didn't agree with Kaep's decision to kneel during the anthem, I don't think that had anything to do with our struggles. Once he got up in front of the team and explained why he was protesting in a very respectful, intellectual way, I think that quelled any ill feelings some may have had.

Now, a lot of the brothers, including myself, already knew what it was off jump, of course. But when he explained that he was doing it because of the ongoing oppression of black people, and elaborated on how we get pulled over for basic traffic offenses and sometimes don't make it home, I think it really helped.

Don't get me wrong; some players still felt the way they felt about it. Some still found it inappropriate because we chose to protest during the national anthem, and they just felt it was disrespectful to the flag. But once Kaep spoke on it to the team, guys who were on the fence got a better understanding, and there was no turmoil, no heated arguments. People just had their own opinions.

The only thing that was different about the whole situation was that the media asked us a lot of questions about it, as opposed to football questions. But I actually don't think that's a bad thing—it brought a lot of spotlight to an important issue for African-Americans during a lost season for the team, an issue that rages on to this day, largely because of President Donald Trump.

When Trump called the protesting players "sons of bitches" in September 2017, there was outrage among many black players, most of whom were like, "Fuck Trump." We were feeling that type of way already, but when he called us out publicly, he put coaches and owners on the spot because they knew that in a league where 70 percent of the players are black, they basically had to defend us. Trump's language was particularly demeaning because athletes get stereotyped as troublemakers. But in reality, many of us—myself included—do lots of work in the community that most people have no clue about.

Even still, I feel the league could have stuck its neck out for us more than it did. Some owners released statements and encouraged team-wide gestures of unity during the anthem the first week after he said it, but that was basically the extent of the support we got.

That said, I think it's huge for players to continue to use their voice, continue to use their platform, and continue to be heard, whether people like it or not. We have this platform and we have to talk about things that make people uncomfortable, because if we don't, who will?

As for me, the 2016 season was my last in San Francisco. I'd had another good season, recording over 100 tackles, and I still had a year left on my deal. But I could see the team was going younger, I knew I didn't want to play on a rebuilding team. So when they asked me to take a pay cut—even when they had like $100 million in cap space—and told me they saw me as the third safety (which meant I wouldn't have a chance to compete for the job), I just went ahead and asked for my release.

But here's what I really liked about a tough situation: the new general manager, John Lynch, is a former player, so he understood why I wanted to move on. Like me, he's as competitive as they come, and he understood why I didn't want to be told before we even got to camp that I wouldn't have a chance to compete for a starting job.

Even still, before he'd grant my request to be released, he asked that I come meet with him in his office so we could chat. During that meeting, I explained my position to him and he explained his position to me, and I left appreciating the respectful way it was handled. It was the way I figured I'd leave Indianapolis, but hey, such is life.

The night I was released, it didn't take long for me to find more work. As soon as my name came across the ticker, my agent got a call from Tampa Bay, which was about to send me a ticket that night. But when I heard from Arizona—whose head coach was Bruce Arians and defensive coordinator was James Boettcher, both of whom used to be with me in Indy—my interest was piqued.

I'd been working out in Phoenix during the offseason since 2007, and I already had masseuses and trainers in the area. The money was right, too (three years and $12 million), and although my family would stay behind in the Bay Area for a while—we were building our forever home in Charlotte and I didn't want my family to move twice in two years—San Francisco was close, only a 90-minute flight away.

So with little hesitation, I agreed to a three-year, $12 million deal with the Cardinals in March 2017, completely unaware that the ensuing distance between myself and my young family would be the very thing that helped me crystallize and capture my rules for success once and for all.

EPILOGUE

During a quiet afternoon this summer at our Bay Area rental, Sam and I were sitting on a couch, watching television, when all of a sudden, she turned to me and smiled. We had just finished flipping through photos of the brand-new house we were building in Charlotte, which was set to be done in early August, and Sam was feeling a little reflective.

"Babe, I never would have imagined we'd have a house that's paid off, both kids' college tuition paid for, by the age of 34," she said. "We can do whatever we want to do when you retire. What else can you ask for?"

I've spent so much time working my butt off to prove my doubters wrong, I don't typically think like that much, other than the times I speak to high school students. But I was glad Sam did in that moment, because she was right.

Parents always talk about building a legacy for their family and giving their kids something they didn't have, and the truth is, if you ask anyone from our hometowns, there's no doubt we're living the dream. If you could go back to 2005 and talk to our 21-year-old selves at Howard, we would have been thrilled at what would become of our lives.

I think my ability to appreciate the journey—and not get *quite* as caught up in the destination—is the biggest way I've grown since I entered the league in 2006. When you're a 22-year-old NFL player, you're just out there living life and having fun, all while being paid lots of money to hit people and have a good time.

But now, I think, being a 34-year-old man with a wife and two kids, the experiences you have had give you a needed perspective, and the responsibilities of fatherhood—of passing on your name and raising good kids—really hit you. At some point, you realize you're not just living for yourself anymore; people are depending on you.

Siani is five and Ace is two, but they already look so much like me, and when I stare at them, I realize that being a father is a beautiful thing. I take the responsibility seriously, and that's why it was so tough for me to spend the 2017 season away from them in Phoenix. I can see them via FaceTime, which is nice, but the time away from them also makes me think a lot about what my life after football will look like, and I'm not gonna lie—it doesn't look so bad.

Ideally, I'd like to play a few more seasons and retire after the 2020 campaign, giving me 15 years in the league. But even if I don't reach that number, I take pride in knowing that of the 18 safeties who were taken before me in the 2006 NFL Draft, I've had the longest playing career, by far, and I'm the last one standing. I can live with that, knowing that if schools like Ohio State and Virginia Tech could go back to the winter of 2002, they'd probably recruit that scrawny 5-foot-11, 170-pound senior linebacker from Denbigh High School that they once deemed too small. The same can be said for the 31 other NFL teams that passed on me in the draft multiple times.

But old habits die hard, you know, and it's not like I've mellowed out completely. I can't, not with these rules ingrained in my head.

Take my entire stint in Arizona, for instance. When the 49ers released me, I definitely took it personally (Rule No. 3) and had a renewed sense of urgency (Rule No. 1) since I was so motivated to prove them wrong. I ended up signing with Arizona, which was a bet on myself (Rule No. 2) because all they promised me was a chance to compete for a starting job.

And, when I didn't earn a starting job for the first time in my career—the coaching staff opted to start a pair of younger veterans, Tyrann Mathieu and Tyvon Branch—I didn't pout, and I didn't make excuses or explanations (Rule No. 4).

Instead, I just made the best of it and took the role they gave me—nickel safety—and ran with it, finishing the season with a career-high five interceptions. It was exactly what Sam advised me to do when I told her about the coaching staff's decision before the season, again proving the importance of having good people in your corner (Rule No. 5),

And when Mathieu left during free agency in March, that opened the door for me to secure a starting job again under a new coaching staff. I told myself I was going to grab that shit by the neck—there was no way I was getting complacent (Rule No. 6) with an opportunity like that in front of me—and I'm happy to report that in August, I indeed secured a starting job for the 2018 season.

And finally, I plan on standing for what I believe in (Rule No. 7) again this fall, as the issues of police brutality and social injustice continue to boil over in the black community. The NFL instituted a new policy in April, giving players the option to stay in the locker room if they don't want to honor the flag, but whatever I choose to do, I'll be sure that people know, one way or another, that my feelings on this issue have not changed.

See how so much of my life is governed by these rules? Even when my playing career is over, and I move on to managing my businesses, I'm sure these pillars will lay the foundation, as people often underestimate football players' business savvy. I know there will be some people saying, "OK, there's no way 'Toine can be a successful businessman," and I can't wait to prove them wrong down the road.

But if I'm being honest, the thing I'm most looking forward to in the future is not only teaching these rules for success to my kids, but also being able to watch them accomplish their dreams using these rules as a guide.

For my son, one of the rules I will definitely stress early on is No. 4, "no excuses, no explanations." Teen boys tend to want to explain away all their mistakes, but I want him to learn the importance of being a man of your word and getting the job done, no matter what. And on the occasions where you fall short and do something you're not supposed to do, you simply have to own up to it and take the "L." But most importantly, you have to learn from that situation. I'll definitely be teaching that to my daughter as well.

My hope is in 35 years or so, I'll be able to sit back, look at my kids and grandchildren and say I set up something perfect for my family—a legacy. I always imagine that moment of satisfaction coming on a family trip, where it's me, Sam and my adult kids having a drink, laughing and playing cards. And when they leave, my wife and I will look at each other and say we've created something beautiful.

But all that's a long way away, and I know it. In the meantime, there are so many goals left to accomplish—one of which, believe it or not, was fulfilled with the publishing of this book. Who would have ever thought lil' ol' 'Toine from Newport News, the high school linebacker that no one wanted, would one day author a book?

My entire goal for this project was to write something honest, something that you could read fairly quickly and come away with some lessons that you can apply to your life, no matter your vocation. I also hope that reading about all these times where people doubted me—and I achieved anyway—inspire you to remember the underlying key behind all these rules, which is that nothing in this world beats persistence. When in doubt, push forward—that's what I'll be doing for the rest of my life.

Because while I'm proud of everything I've accomplished, I'm not done proving doubters wrong. As long as there are people in the world, there will be people who wonder whether I can do whatever I've set out to do, and I can't wait to throw that on my motivational fire. It will all make for good material for book No. 2, which will be coming down the road because, I promise you, I'm not done yet.

ANTOINE BETHEA, a defensive team captain for the Arizona Cardinals, has played 13 seasons in the National Football League. A Super Bowl champion with the 2006 Indianapolis Colts, the three-time Pro-Bowler has clearly distinguished himself as one of the NFL's top safeties and a role model on and off the field.

Bethea launched the Safe Coverage Foundation in 2010, a non-profit committed to giving students the resources they need to gain access to higher education. Bethea is also the vice president of Shutdown Academy 757, a non-profit designed to empower boys and girls and help them reach their potential.

Born July 27, 1984, in Savannah, Georgia, Bethea was raised in Virginia. Bethea excelled in academics and athletics in high school and went on to attend Howard University, where he eventually received his bachelor's degree in criminal justice. During his time in college, Bethea set multiple team records and was named to the Black College All-American Team three years in a row. He also earned All-Mid-Eastern Athletic Conference (MEAC) honors three years in a row.

Bethea was drafted in the 6th round (207th overall) of the 2006 NFL Draft by the Indianapolis Colts and went on to have a stellar rookie season for the Super Bowl XLI champions, starting 14 games for the NFL's No. 2 pass defense. Bethea received many awards during his eight years with the Colts, including the Ed Block Courage Award in 2012 and 2013 Community Man of the Year.

In 2014, after an impactful career with the Colts, Bethea signed a four-year deal with the San Francisco 49ers. In his first season with the 49ers, Bethea made the Pro Bowl and was voted Team MVP by his teammates. The next year, Bethea was also inducted into the MEAC Hall of Fame.

In March 2017, after three strong seasons with the 49ers, Bethea signed a three-year contract with the Arizona Cardinals. In Bethea's first year with the Cardinals, he recorded 57 tackles and a career-high five interceptions in 15 games, and in February 2018, he was chosen to be the inaugural recipient of the Black College Football Pro Player of the Year Award, which is presented by the NFL Players Association.

Bethea continues to impress and lead his teammates on the field, while inspiring countless others off it. An outstanding father and community member, Bethea remains committed to being the best man and player he can be.

Terez Paylor is an award-winning sportswriter who covers the National Football League for Yahoo Sports. Paylor, a Pro Football Hall of Fame voter, joined Yahoo in 2018 after 12 years at The Kansas City Star, where he covered the Kansas City Chiefs and the NFL.

CPSIA information can be obtained
at www.ICGtesting.com
Printed in the USA
BVHW030331240120
570221BV00012B/6